"A must read for all who want to better understand the power shift to Asia"
Dr. Gene Ward, *former Country Director, East Timor, U.S. Peace Corps*

"…more objective than…Washington."
Ray Burghardt, *Chair, American Institute in Taiwan, and Director, East-West Center, Hawaii*

"constructed on…man-to-man dialog"
Hotaeck Hwang, *Chief editorial writer and columnist of Dongailbo (leading newspaper in Korea since 1920)*

Random Views of Asia
from the Mid-Pacific

William E. Sharp, Jr.

Savant Books and Publications
Honolulu, HI, USA
2012

Published in the USA by Savant Books and Publications
2630 Kapiolani Blvd #1601
Honolulu, HI 96826
http://www. savantbooksandpublications. com

Printed in the USA

Edited by Zachary M. Oliver
Cover Art and Design by Kristen Arbuckle

Copyright 2012 William E. Sharp, Jr. All rights reserved. No part of this work may be reproduced without the prior written permission of the author.

13-digit ISBN: 978-0-9832861-1-0
10-digit ISBN: 0983286116

This book is primarily non-fictional. Ahough the information conveyed comes from different sources, every effort has been made to make this work as accurate as possible. However, there may remain errors, both typographical and in content.

The author and publisher have neither liability nor responsibility to any person or entity with respect to any loss or damage caused, or alleged to have been caused, directly or indirectly, by the information conveyed in this book.

Dedication

To my father, the late William E. Sharp, Sr. and my mother, Margaret S. Sharp for their love, support, and devotion.

Acknowledgment

No book would be accomplished without the help of others. My good friend, Mike Dane gave me the inspiration for *Random Views of Asia from the Mid-Pacific,* and my lifelong partner, Xiaodong Qiao, lent her unconditional support and enthusiasm in addition to technical assistance. *Honolulu Star-Advertiser* Vice-President and Editor Frank Bridgewater permitted me use of material published in the former *Honolulu Star-Bulletin.*

Random Views of Asia from the Mid-Pacific

TABLE OF CONTENTS

Forward	i
Chapter One - Asia	1
Chapter Two - China	35
Chapter Three - Tibet	125
Chapter Four - Taiwan	129
Chapter Five - Korea	167
Chapter Six - Japan	199
Chapter Seven - India	219
Chapter Eight - Central Asia	233
Chapter Nine - Vietnam	239
Chapter Ten - Russia	257
Afterward	265
About the Author	269

Random Views of Asia from the Mid-Pacific

William E. Sharp, Jr.

Forward

During the last decade, the focus of American foreign and defense policy has been almost exclusively on the Middle East and Central Asia. With its two most vivid expressions the wars in Iraq and Afghanistan, our military and much of our diplomatic corps has been preoccupied with the War on Terror. Meanwhile, China has continued its rise, evolving into a significant challenge in the East.

To date, China has appeared reluctant to play too strong a role far from its own shores. This is now changing as China steps into the limelight on global issues, and as the rest of the world begins encouraging Chinese participation and increasingly seeks its leadership. At the same time, China's military modernization and expansion—as well as its growing wealth—have given it new clout in pursuing its regional interest, a situation that does not bode well for stability in the region. The incremental increase in tensions in the South China Sea, now emerging as a designated "core interest" for China, bring new tensions with Southeast Asia—particularly with Vietnam. The long-term relationship with India remains tenuous, given China's military and political relationship with Pakistan and several unresolved border disputes. The Russian Federation's interest in cooperation has waned as the prospects for development of the Chinese energy market have floundered, and as Chinese reverse-engineering of Russian military platforms has complicated the defense relationship.

China's rise also presents a unique challenge to the United States, the nation that has been the preeminent power and stabilizing force in the Pacific since 1945. While China and the U.S. have broad and deep commercial ties, the relationship is peppered with trade friction and squabbles over currency. While American military power is still without peer in the region, China's anti-access and denial strategies are threatening U.S. forces in new and challenging ways. China is also modernizing its thinking, building advanced cyberspace and space-based capabilities, with the clear intention of challenging American predominance in the Pacific.

Important as the China relationship has become, however, U.S policy in Asia has become too focused on China to the exclusion and determent of other important relationships. Over the past decade, America has had a China policy rather than an Asia policy, and that has eroded relationships and undermined important opportunities for the U.S. in the region. Other Asian countries have also been changing fast with growing economic and military muscle. In addition, there seems to be awareness of what can be accomplished if they act together—such as during the Association of Southeast Asian Nations' recent push back on China's South China Sea grab.

There is no doubt that Asia has arrived, and that the region will grow ever more important during the next decade. But the emergence of Asia has not happened overnight, and in this book, Bill Sharp taps into a wealth of insight garnered from his academic and journalistic endeavors to map the string of important issues that has impacted the region and will continue to affect its future.

Bill's thoughtful coverage is coupled with important and relevant historic and institutional tie-ins. To properly appreciate why countries act the way they do, it is imperative that issues are understood in their historical context. An excellent example is latent friction between China and Japan that exists as a consequence of Japanese fascism and the war with China from 1937 to 1945.

Strong personalities are also vitally important in shaping interactions and relationships. In this book, Bill's focus on key relationships, such as the one between George W. Bush and Japan's Junichiro Koizumi who made a deal to move the Futenma base to a more discreet location, help us better understand important developments that laid the groundwork for breakthroughs in bilateral relations. While this deal has since foundered, it remains an important representation of the significance of personal relationships between principals and what can be achieved through them.

Ultimately, the network of interconnecting trade routes, historic relationships, disputed territories, and legacy grievances create a web of contradictions and challenges. Bill does an excellent job unraveling some of these dynamics and examining their impact on the prospect for continued American engagement in the region. This book would give anyone with a keen interest in international affairs a head start in understanding the forces that are shaping Asia.

Rupert Hammond-Chambers, President, U.S.-Taiwan Business Council, November 4, 2011

William E. Sharp, Jr.

Random Views of Asia from the Mid-Pacific

William E. Sharp, Jr.

Chapter One

ASIA

America in Asia: 2025
Honolulu, February 12, 2006

"President Bush is obsessed with Middle East policy," said *New York Times* columnist David Brooks in a recent Public Broadcasting System interview. However, America has major economic and strategic concerns in Northeast and Southeast Asia. Since the defeat of Japan in 1945, America has been the primary foreign power in the region. Its interests have been maintained through security treaties; maintenance of army, navy, and air force bases; foreign direct investment; preferential trade agreements' and cultural and academic exchanges. The goal of U.S. policy in both Northeast and Southeast Asia during the last sixty years has been to stop the spread of communism, which was meant to stop the rise of China.

Until China rejoined the world in 1978, U.S. policy was successful. The United States had a strong relationship with both South Korea and Japan in Northeast Asia. Both Japan and the United States were very influential in Southeast Asia. However, as the

Chinese economy began to grow, strengthen its military and invigorate its diplomacy, challenges to American supremacy in Northeast and Southeast Asia are more apparent, more successful, and more frequent.

During the 1997-98 Asian Financial Crisis, China showed sympathetic understanding toward Thailand, Indonesia, and Malaysia by offering financial assistance. Asian nations began to talk about creating a source of large-scale financing independent from the United States dominated International Monetary Fund (IMF). Strains in the South Korean-U.S. relationship had been mounting for years. As South Korean attitudes toward the United States continued to shift, China and South Korea established formal diplomatic relations in 1992. Before long, China became an important market for South Korea.

In 2005, the United States redeployed 3,600 troops from Korea to fight in Iraq with no apparent intention to replace them, and plans to continue drawing down troops to 25,000 by 2008.

In September 1991, the Filipino national legislature voted not to extend leases on land housing the U.S. military. After the withdrawal of the U.S. Navy from Subic Bay and the U.S. Air Force from Clark Air Base, China began to improve its relations with the Philippines by offering low-cost loans.

In Southeast Asia, China's relations with Thailand have soared. Today, Thailand is crowded with Chinese tourists. China also built great influence in Cambodia, Laos, and Burma. Vietnam seeks a good relationship with the United States, but the Vietnamese Politburo's pre-eminent foreign policy concern is to maintain good relations with China. More recently, China has achieved major diplomatic breakthroughs with India, the world's second-most populous country, and Indonesia, the world's largest Muslim country, which also is oil rich.

In the course of improving its relations with its neighbors, a fundamental shift in Chinese diplomatic thinking has appeared. Traditionally, post-1949 China sought diplomatic relations with other countries on the basis of bilateral relations. It has eschewed any form of alliance or multilateral or regional relationship. However, China now appreciates the utility of multilateral relations as it strives to become the leading regional power in Northeast and Southeast Asia, which it feels will ensure its security and continued economic growth.

As the diplomatic standoff over North Korean nuclear weapons between North Korea and the United States intensified, China offered to host the Six-Party Talks (SPT), inviting Japan, South Korea, North Korea, Russia, and the United States to work out an agreement to guarantee that North Korea would halt the development of nuclear weapons. The SPT have yet to prove any conclusive result other than having embellished China's diplomatic credentials.

Shortly after the last formal session of the SPT though, China surprisingly broached a proposal to establish a regional security system in which all powers, including the United States, would participate. Details of the proposal were not made known. However, the establishment of such a regional security system with all parties ostensibly supporting the goal of regional security on an equal basis likely would dilute the influence of the United States in Northeast Asian security. As such, it would create a pretext for a further withdrawal of U.S. troops from South Korea and Japan, leaving resident regional security member China in a more influential position.

Since the end of the Vietnam War, Asia has experienced the growth of multilateral regional organizations that are concerned with both economic and security issues. These include the Association of Southeast Asian Nations, ASEAN + 1, ASEAN + 3, ASEAN + 6, the ASEAN Regional Forum (ARF), and the Asia Pacific Economic Cooperation (APEC). Although not a member of ASEAN, the United States participates in the ARF. It was not invited to the first East Asian Summit on December 14, 2005, in Kuala Lumpur, Malaysia. Surprising to many, Russia was invited, albeit as an observer. At the same time, China has become increasingly active in ASEAN, using its newly acquired economic strength, from which many Asian nations have benefited, to promote its leadership. The ASEAN + 1 agreement, signed in 2004, liberalizes trade between ASEAN and China. Signed by national leaders at the conclusion of the summit, the Kuala Lumpur Declaration on the East Asian Summit (KLDEAS) committed signatories to "fostering strategic dialogue and promoting cooperation in political and security issues." Economically, the KLDEAS promised "development, financial stability, energy security, economic integration."

As a renewed Asian economic giant, Japan is an important player in most Asian multilateral organizations. Thus, Japan can use its participation and influence to help promote common interests it holds with the United States. However, it cannot be assumed that Japan and the United States will always be as close as they seem to have gotten. China would certainly like to separate Japan from the United States, since it realizes that Japan's influence in Asia and the world is enhanced by its relationship with America. It is true that given the acerbic state of Sino-Japanese relations that Japan is currently relying more on U.S. security guarantees. The militaries of Japan and the United States have achieved a higher level of equipment interoperability and a more closely integrated command structure. However, as Robyn Lim, Professor of International Relations at Nanzan University in Nagoya, Japan, and a former analyst for Australia's Office of National Assessments argues in, "The U.S. Puts Japan on Probation," in the November 2005 issue of the *Far Eastern Economic Review*, a closer U.S. relationship with Japan might lead to the United States getting involved in more disputes between China and Japan. An example might be resolution over the Senkaku Islands (Diaoyutai in Chinese).

As long as Prime Minister Koizumi Junichiro remains in office, U.S.-Japanese relations should remain stable; however, he is expected to step down in late 2006. While he has been popular with many Japanese, other Japanese and non-Japanese experts feel that he has unnecessarily exacerbated Japan's relations with China by continually visiting Yasukuni Shrine, where the remains of those who ravaged China during World War II are enshrined.

Many Japanese businessmen are eager to improve relations with China. After all, it was the vitality of the Chinese market that was so important in restoring Japanese economic power and is seen as a source of future economic growth. Koizumi's cabinet has been unyielding in its support for Taiwan; a new leader will appoint his own cabinet. Potential future Japanese leaders have indicated their willingness to be more flexible in dealing with China. In some respects, the United States would like to see a better Sino-Japanese relationship; on the other hand, an unwritten principle of U.S. policy toward the two Asian giants is to prevent them from colluding too closely. Combining the economic and organizational efficiency of Japan with the energy and cheap labor of China would be to the strategic and economic disadvantage of the United States.

During 2005, the United States experienced a trade deficit of nearly $200 billion with China and a $75 billion trade deficit with Japan. When the United States first began to experience large trade deficits with Japan in the 1980s, economists argued that deficits were not as big of a problem as some suggested. After all, imports gave consumers more choice. Important voices such as former Federal Reserve Board Chairman Alan Greenspan have begun to warn that the United States cannot indefinitely sustain such trade deficits, and there is a growing U.S. concern that Asian trade partners do not play by World

Trade Organization rules.

An editorial in the January 14, 2006 issue of the *Economist* warns about America's trade deficit. To avoid political interference and trade disputes emanating from the United States and the European Union, as the economies of these Asian countries continue to grow, these new powerhouses will adopt economic growth policies based on domestic demand, rather than export driven economic growth. In 2006, the gross national product of Asia will grow by 6.7 percent, according to Christopher Hill, U.S. Assistant Secretary of State for East Asian and Pacific Affairs; a view backed up by statistics published by the United Nations. In other words, access to the U.S. market will be of less importance to Asian nations.

While the United States continues to galvanize its attention on Israel, the newly elected Palestinian government, Iraq, Syria, and Iran, it also will need to give greater attention to areas in its own backyard such as Bolivia, Venezuela, and Brazil, where its traditional diplomatic and economic influence is weakening and China's presence is growing. At the same time, China will continue to promote both a regional security system and block trade through regional multilateral organizations. With a regional security system in place and economies less dependent on the United States, its role in Northeast and Southeast Asia will be greatly diminished.

Regional reconfiguration will not be easily wrought. There will be periodic economic, political, and other policy differences between countries with competing interests. Some nations will distance themselves farther from the United States than others; yet no country will completely slam its door on a relationship with the United States, if only to preserve a safety valve in the event of Chinese, Japanese, or Sino-Japanese hegemony. China cannot isolate Japan within Asia. More importantly, both nations will have to reach some accommodation to promote their own self-interests in Asia.

To achieve pre-eminence in Northeast and Southeast Asia, China will take a long-term view, exercise great patience, be flexible, and maintain the ability to live with ambiguity and contradiction, not to mention adroitly handle different problems as they surface.

Bush Comes Back Empty-Handed
Honolulu, December 14, 2005

Just as National Security Adviser Stephen J. Hadley allowed when asked by journalists, President Bush's November 16-21, 2005 trip to Asia held little expectation of any major breakthroughs.

America's strongest bilateral relationship with an Asian country is with Japan, to which the growing Koizumi-Bush relationship has added much. Bush's mention of how their fathers had both fought in the Pacific during World War II and how their two sons now stood as leaders of the two most economically powerful countries in the globe lent a warm fuzzy quality to the close U.S.-Japanese relationship. Nevertheless, the two-year Japanese ban against importing U.S. beef was not rescinded regardless of Bush's efforts to normalize trade.

In a Kyoto speech, Bush lauded President Harry Truman's enlightened policies during the post World War II U.S. occupation of Japan. The President contended such policies brought Japan into the family of democratic nations and helped to propel Japan into the ranks of wealthy, developed nations. As a result, Japan was a model for the rest of Asia to follow. Certainly there are lessons to learn from occupation policies; however, mention of Truman and discussion of the occupation continue to be very politically risky and extremely sensitive topics in Japan. After all, it was during Truman's presidency that the U.S. dropped nuclear bombs on Hiroshima and Nagasaki. The occupation was the only time that Japan has been occupied by a foreign power. The Japanese themselves feel ill at ease discussing it. Just at a time when China holds itself as a model for others to follow, Beijing could not have been more pleased with Bush's remarks.

In fact, Sino-Japanese relations are at perhaps their lowest level since the countries re-established formal diplomatic relations in 1972. A key reason for this state of affairs is the Japanese cabinet's strong support for Taiwan, a Japanese colony until the end of World War II. While in Japan, Bush's trumpeting Taiwan's democratic evolution and thriving economy could hardly have gone over well with the Beijing leadership, although he did reconfirm America's one-China policy.

The first international leader to visit President Bush after he was first elected was former South Korean President and Nobel Prize winner Kim Dae-jung. The meeting did not go well with political neophyte Bush lecturing Kim about dealing with North Korea. Unlike Bush, Kim believed that the way to deal with the North was to interact with it. Kim's successor, President Roh Moo-hyun and Bush do not maintain a close relationship largely owing to South Korean and American differences on how to approach North Korea and the growing quest for national identity among younger Koreans. Like his predecessor, Roh prefers a more patient, less aggressive approach than does the U.S. However, both the U.S. and South Korea do want to see the denuclearization of North Korea. President Bush went to Korea to attend the Asia-Pacific Economic Cooperation (APEC) summit of twenty-one world leaders with the goal of achieving trade liberalization. Hosted by President Roh, the summit yielded no economic advantage for the U.S. No sooner had both presidents promised to improve bilateral relations than the South Korean government announced a proposal to withdraw one third of its 3,200 troops from Iraq, the last thing Bush wanted from any coalition partner.

Immediately upon arrival in Beijing, Bush proceeded to the Gangwashi Church for services. Such imagery undoubtedly would work well with Bush's core political constituency back in the U.S., but it was certainly not the right way to build relations with a country deeply skeptical of Western religion, even though the church was government-sanctioned. Given America's traditional advocacy of human rights, the Chinese government has typically released a few incarcerated human rights activists before the visit of a U.S. president or other high level U.S. representative. However, this was not the case during Bush's visit to China. In fact, thirty protesters who wanted to meet with the President were arrested. Many observers concluded that President Hu Jintao, a former head of the Central Party School and First Secretary of the politically discontent Tibet Autonomous Region, was cracking down on any form of political dissent.

To address America's exploding trade deficit with China, estimated to run $200 billion for 2005, U.S. policy has sought to persuade China to float the yuan (the Chinese unit of currency) with only limited results. The U.S. has sought enforcement of intellectual property rights concerning the piracy of movies and software. Trade officials presented the Chinese government with a list of twenty-five factories that reproduced U.S.-made DVDs. The Chinese government has yet to implement any corrective measures.

Much was made of China's decision to purchase seventy Boeing jets at a price tag of $4 billion. However, China needed to make some gesture of attempting to reduce the trade deficit, as China was manufacturing part of Boeing's fuselages. Shortly afterwards, China announced its interest in buying a large order of aircraft from Airbus.

Bush's twelve-hour stay in Mongolia was to express

appreciation to the Mongolian government for sending 140 Mongolian troops to Iraq. Moreover, it was recognition of Mongolia's democratization and difficult transformation to a market economy.

While not reaping any tangible results, some view the trip as an attempt to restore American influence and soft power lost in Northeast Asia by reminding the world of Japan's, South Korea's, and Taiwan's democratic freedoms and material comfort. All were achieved with U.S. economic assistance and security guarantees. Perhaps one day Mongolia will similarly benefit.

The View from Camp Smith
Honolulu, October 12, 2008

Started in 1947 by order of President Truman, the U.S. Pacific Command (PACOM) is the oldest and largest U.S. unified command. Covering one-half of the globe or thirty-six countries from the West Coast of the U.S. to the East Coast of Africa and from the Arctic to Antarctica, there are approximately 300,000 military personnel from the navy, army, air force, and marines that come under the control of PACOM. The command has approximately 141 ships, 39 submarines, 360 air force planes, 900 naval aircraft, 250 army aircraft, and 600 marine aircraft. Economically, 38% or $1.1 trillion U.S. dollars worth of trade took place in the Asian-Pacific arena in 2006. Future gains in U.S. trade are likely given that Asia is fastest growing economic region in the world.

Given the enormity of PACOM's area of responsibility and the assets it controls, the position of Commander PACOM is a highly coveted four-star billet. Admiral Timothy J. Keating, a 1971 U.S. Naval Academy graduate, assumed command in March 2007 coming from his position as Commander of the North American Aerospace Defense Command and the U.S. Northern Command.

"In line with the National Defense Strategy of 2008, PACOM is fully prepared to fight and win the nation's wars," declared Admiral Keating. However, its mission is not a purely military one. As proud as he is of PACOM's battle readiness, Keating is equally proud of PACOM's role as a good citizen discharging humanitarian assistance. The naval hospital ship USS *Mercy* has played an active role in the Asian-Pacific arena dispensing medical services. PACOM ships, aircraft, and personnel provided disaster relief during the Indian Ocean earthquake in 2004. And earlier this year (2008), U.S. Air Force C-17 cargo aircraft delivered supplies to China in the aftermath of massive earthquakes and after shocks.

Keating feels strongly that the American leadership style does not always need to have the U.S. out in front leading. The U.S. can lead from within, outside, or behind, Keating declared in a question and answer session in May at the Japan Society of New York. In other words, the U.S. can lend personnel or materiel support to a multilateral activity, but it doesn't need to play a dominant role.

Admiral Keating's greatest worry is the potential threat from China. Because of a lack of transparency, one of the greatest challenges—if not frustrations—is reading and comprehending the People's Liberation Army's (PLA) intentions. According to the Washington Post, Jiang Enzhu, Chinese National People's spokesperson, said that China's military budget increased by 15.8 percent from 2003 to 2007. This year it will increase by 17.6 percent. Since the budget is scattered in different areas, the actual increase could be larger. Determining the exact size of the budget is of vital importance to the U.S. China prefers to parry U.S. inquiries about the growth in the military budget by claiming that additional budget is necessary to upgrade the quality of life for PLA members in order to prevent them from taking higher paying jobs in China's sizzling private sector. Keating acknowledges that PLA living conditions do not match those enjoyed by U.S. military members; however, skepticism remains.

What are the PLA's strengths? Keating quickly pointed out China's population of over 1.3 billion offers a huge source for recruitment, and the PLA enjoys wide government support from the Central Military Commission. The Second Artillery, China's strategic missile force, with both nuclear and conventional weapons and the PLA Navy's sixty-five submarines are most certainly a worry to anyone who might have to militarily confront China. Admiral Keating, to his credit, readily admitted that: In the event of an emergency, additional submarines will be needed and it will take a while to get them to the Pacific from the East Coast.

The Chinese clearly want to have an aircraft carrier, and there are a number of Chinese magazines and news stories devoted to discussing the addition. The admiral said, "There is no greater a symbol of national sovereignty and national pride than an aircraft carrier sailing into a foreign port with its national ensign blowing in the breeze." A seasoned aviator with over 5,000 flight hours and 1,200 carrier landings, he adds, "Operating a carrier is not as easy as it looks." Thus, it will take China sometime to properly train the hundreds of personnel it takes to manage a carrier in an effective combat fashion.

The PLA requires serious attention, yet it does have weaknesses. It has improved in certain tactics and procedures, but it still has problems in command and control. Theoretically, the PLA is a unified force blending together China's land, air, and naval forces into one. However, certain inter-service rivalries exist. The U.S. has lots of experience in joint and coalition operations; China doesn't. Admiral Keating said, "World scale operations are hard for the Chinese to get used to."

Admiral Keating pointed out that a significant PLA weakness is China's underdeveloped non-commissioned officer (NCO) corps which is not as experienced as the U.S.'s. As a result, the PLA's execution of military operations is not as good as America's. Chinese NCOs' careers also suffer from lack of a clear career path.

The admiral exclaimed,"The U.S. must not ignore China!" Despite our concern for humanitarian operations, U.S. military power should not be underestimated. He is working to build cooperation and communication between PACOM and the PLA. During his tenure, a military hotline has been put into operation between Washington and the Beijing. He strongly advocates exchange programs that would see more Chinese attending U.S. schools and hopes to conduct limited military operations between the U.S. and China. Both exchanges and joint operations would allow the Chinese to see how far ahead the U.S. military is.

He understands that China wishes to protect its national interests just as the U.S. does, and both countries have a vital interest in keeping sea lanes of communication open. However, he emphasizes, "That to go beyond or behind [militarily] the U.S. is not beneficial. It is not useful to try to catch the U.S. The U.S. is not hegemonic." During one of his two trips to China, the admiral was approached by a Chinese flag officer who suggested that once China acquired its aircraft carrier, China should take the Pacific west of Hawaii and the U.S. take the Pacific east of Hawaii. The admiral thanked the Chinese officer for his offer, pointing out that it was more than likely to be declined. "The Pacific Ocean is big enough for everyone," said Keating. Clearly, he did not want an antagonistic relationship to evolve. Admiral Keating was cautiously optimistic about developing relations with the PLA.

William E. Sharp, Jr.

Create a New U.S. Approach to NE Asia
Honolulu, January 13, 2008

Presidential debate after presidential debate, photo op after photo op, TV interview after TV interview, yet there still has only been little substantive discussion or few policy prescriptions for Northeast Asia (NEA) from most leading candidates. Meanwhile, China has emerged as a key Asian regional and international power that has created a new calculus of power in NEA with which America has not come to terms.

U.S. Asian policy during the Cold War sought to contain China to prevent its revolutionary Marxist influence from spreading to neighboring countries. In NEA, the U.S. built strong bilateral relationships with the Republic of Korea and Japan. The U.S. guaranteed Korean and Japanese security by concluding mutual defense treaties with both countries. To bring further political stability and economic growth to its key NEA allies, the U.S. threw open its markets to Korea and Japan. Physically secure and with growing economies, the U.S. helped to create burgeoning democracies in both countries.

Nevertheless, the emphasis has always been on bilateral relations, and there was no attempt to build any kind of multilateral regional security or economic apparatus.

In 1978, China opened to the world, and in 1991, the Soviet Union dissolved bringing with it the end of the Cold War.

Since the founding of the People's Republic of China in 1949, China pursued international relations solely on the basis of bilateral relationships. However, after actively rendering economic assistance during the Asian Financial Crisis of 1997 to 1998, it broke out of its bilateral mode to pursue a foreign policy based on multilateralism. Most speeches by General Secretary of the Communist Party of China, Hu Jintao or other leading party members trumpet the approach.

Chinese advocacy of multilateralism is not simply rhetorical. One only has to look at the great degree of attention China pays to Asia's premier multilateral organization, the Association of Southeast Asian Nations. Unlike the Asia Pacific Economic Cooperation, where the U.S. is a member, China is maneuvering along with Russia to create the Shanghai Cooperation Organization to stymie U.S. influence in Central Asia. China's desire to create a regional security apparatus in NEA could, in the long run, be used to diminish the U.S. security posture in NEA.

Korea and Japan wish to maintain their security relationships anchored in the mutual defense treaties with the U.S.; furthermore, the U.S. market is still crucial to them. However, the Koreans and Japanese don't always agree with the U.S., and the Chinese market is more important to them than is the U.S. market. Thus, at times it will be more advantageous, from the standpoint of Korean and Japanese national interests, to cooperate with China and at other times with the U.S. Even though South Korean President-elect Lee Myung-bak has a world view that promises to be more in line with Washington's than incumbent President Roh's, South Korea cannot be expected to always follow the U.S. lead. The same is true for Japan where Prime Minister Yasuo Fukuda's primary external concern will be building relations with Asia, especially China and South Korea.

Mr. Terashima Jitsuro, President of the Mitsui Strategic Research Institute, says, "Asia will account for 50% of global GDP by 2050." As NEA economies grow and as the dollar continues to depreciate, intra-Asian trading will become more and more important to NEA countries, and the U.S. market less and less. This means that NEA nations will become less likely to follow the lead of the U.S. and respond positively to U.S. concerns.

NEA multilateral economic growth focusing on China, Japan, South Korea, North Korea, the Russian Far East, and Mongolia continues to receive more and more attention. Both South Korea and Japan have a number of organizations devoted to promoting such growth and more serious and frequent meetings are being held to create a NEA Development Bank in the near future. In the wake of the Six-Party Talks, we are bound to see more serious attempts to create a viable NEA regional security organization. There is increasing interest in creating an organization that might borrow some of the architecture and modus operandi of the Organization for Security and Co-operation (OSCE) in Europe. The OSCE provides members with a multilateral regional organization to address economic and security issues.

Adjusting to a multilaterally focused NEA where it

would not be the preeminent power will be difficult for the U.S.; however, the trend continues to gain momentum. In recent issues of *Foreign Affairs*, Presidential candidates John McCain, Hillary Clinton, and Barack Obama *are* on record favoring a multilateral, regional approach. To turn the situation to its advantage, the U.S. should now vigorously promote its own viable notions of effective multilateral economic and security organizations.

During the next administration, Washington needs to remember that there are vital parts of the world other than just the Middle East and countries that demand just as much—if not more—attention than Iraq, Iran, and Afghanistan. How creatively and flexibly the U.S. handles its foreign policy in NEA promises to have a significant impact on America's future prosperity and global leadership.

Ever a Mirage - Northeast Asian Regionalization
Honolulu, July 8, 2008

It's an oddity of East Asian international politics, that the most vibrant multilateral organization in the region is the Association of Southeast Asian Nations (ASEAN). Wealthier Northeast Asian nations, China, South Korea, and Japan, are most certainly concerned with influencing ASEAN, yet Northeast Asia (NEA) lacks any equivalent organization. The potential clearly exists for both NEA regional economic and security cooperation involving China, South and North Korea, Japan, Russia, and Mongolia. Nevertheless, a history of animosity, disparate cultural values, institutional barriers, and security concerns has impeded any tangible progress in regional integration that could yield economic growth and the reduction of armed threat.

The Six-Party Talks, involving China, the Koreas, Japan, Russia, and the U.S., at long last appear to be making progress in the denuclearization of North Korea. Optimists hope that denuclearization will create more economic cooperation between NEA nations, and there is even talk about creating a NEA Development Bank. Moreover, there is clear Chinese and South Korean interest in morphing the Seven Party Talks (SPT) into a regional security apparatus.

Pursuit of either regional economic or security cooperation faces daunting challenges. China and Japan are locked into a struggle for regional supremacy that contributes to NEA instability. China was the dominate player in East Asia until Japan usurped China's position with its victory in the Sino-Japanese War of 1895. The Japanese invasion of China during World War II and China's insistence that Japan has yet to adequately atone for its atrocities remain a flashpoint in the Sino-Japanese relationship. What is more, China holds that unacceptable U.S. intrusion into the region is anchored by close U.S.-Japanese relations. For its part, Japan is deeply suspicious of China's long-term intentions against a background of burgeoning Chinese economic, military, and diplomatic influence. Strong Japanese support for Taiwan and territorial claim to the Diaoyutai (Chinese) or the Senkakushima (Japanese) Islands hamper the relationship.

Both Koreas clearly remember the period of Japanese colonialism and share with China similarly nightmarish memories of World War II. The Chinese market is especially important to South Korea and helps to balance its huge trade deficit with Japan. China and South Korea have shared a very similar negotiating position in the SPT, yet well informed South Korean observers, who asked not to be named, remain mistrustful of China. Despite North Korean dependence on China for fuel and food, state propaganda debunks China for abandoning Communism and shows little appreciation for Chinese material or diplomatic support.

Furthermore, some South Koreans feel that the Japanese don't consider them as equals. Others feel that America favors the U.S.-Japanese relationship to the U.S.-South Korean relationship. The recent flaring of a sovereignty dispute over the Dokdo (Korean) or Takeshima (Japanese) Islands only intensifies negative feelings. As for North Korea, periodic Japanese government interruption of cash transfers by Koreans living in Japan to relatives in North Korea and the suspension of passenger ship service between the two countries produce venomous propaganda. North Korean missile launches over Japan and failure to disclose the fate of Japanese abductees have contributed to calls for a more aggressive, less constitutionally bound Japanese military.

Next to Sino-Japanese competition for pre-eminence, the division of Korea, in the geographic center of NEA, is the most serious obstacle to regional economic or security cooperation. Seen as a land bridge between China and Japan, who at different times have dominated Korea, the country is of vital security interest to both major powers. The Korean peninsula is one of the most heavily armed areas in the world and pits the numerically superior North Korean army against the more technically sophisticated South Korean military supported by 29,000 U.S. troops that the North demands be withdrawn. The South's Sunshine Policy has tried to use food, fuel, and other incentives to get the North to the bargaining table to carry out family reunions, to prevent the Pyongyang regime from economically imploding, causing an economically crippling rush South of refugees, and to stop development of nuclear weapons.

The Russian Far East (RFE) largely constitutes land that China lost control of due to unequal treaties. Nevertheless, Chinese commercial and criminal influence continues to grow in the area and is of key concern to the Russians as the population of the RFE decreases. Russian nationalistic and security concerns squelched Chinese offers to lease and develop the ports of Zarubino and Posyet that would have stimulated economic growth for the RFE and given China's economically struggling landlocked Jilin and Heilongjiang Provinces access to the sea. Perhaps because of Moscow's overriding concern for relations with the U.S. and the European Union, Russia seems to be the least interested party in ramped up regional cooperation although it has held joint military training exercises with China and exports oil to its southern neighbor.

Until Russia and Japan settle the Kurile Island territorial issue, relations will not likely improve.

Sparsely populated with miles and miles of open space and sandwiched in by its former mentor, Russia, to the north and China to the south, Mongolia seeks to guarantee its security. Moreover, impoverished, landlocked Mongolia wants to generate an economy to replace its lost Soviet assistance.

Indeed, the challenging obstacles to regionalization make it a long-term process. The Honolulu-based Northeast Asian Economic Forum, headed by Chairman Dr. Lee-Jay Cho, Emeritus Fellow of the East West Center and supported by the Hawaii Asia Pacific Institute lead by Board Chair and former Governor George R. Ariyoshi, strives to promote regionalization by promoting dialogue, pinpointing bureaucratic procedures that impede regionalization, and advocating that natural gas, oil, and electricity can play an important role in integration.

As challenging as the obstacles are, the economic benefits are huge.

China could gain access to the sea for its northeastern provinces and to RFE natural, mineral, and water resources. Western Japan, considered a less developed part of the country, would experience new economic vitality as a trade hub facing other partners. Japan would more readily acquire Russian natural resources.

In addition to RFE resources, South Korea would gain a valuable train connection to transport its goods to Europe through North Korea and on to the Trans-Siberian Railway. South Korea would benefit from cheap North Korean labor and an expanded market in the North for its goods. North Korea would be given an opportunity to gain more economic self-sufficiency and to make up for the gap in lost Soviet aid. Mongolia could develop transnational rail links obtaining access to seaports that would help it economically rebuild.

Bereft of its Soviet era subsidies and receiving scant attention from Moscow, the RFE is considered Russia's economic basket case despite its resource wealth. Its economy would benefit from economic integration in NEA which will bring it more investment and more of the consumer goods Russians so desperately crave.

Countries sharing mutual economic benefit normally have a special interest in maintaining peace and stability.

And, what about the U.S.? The end of the Cold War and the rise of China have made it difficult for the U.S. to adhere to bilaterally based diplomacy in NEA as South Korea and Japan consider other forms of interaction with the U.S. While speeches by leading Chinese cadre always promote multilateralism and suggest there would be an American role in any regional security arrangement, America worries that it is a Trojan horse designed to give China time to build economic and military influence that could muscle the U.S. out of NEA. However, given its own military power, capital assets, technological creativity, and ravenous market, it's unlikely the U.S. would be completely sidelined; it would be a far more equal partner who could witness a far less dangerous, more economically robust region. The challenge for the U.S. is, most assuredly, dealing with a changing NEA.

Creating a New Economic Face for Northeast Asia
Toyama, Japan, November 11, 2007

Long held great hopes for bringing economic prosperity to parts of Northeast Asia (NEA) that economic development has not fully embraced were advanced at the 16th annual meeting of the Honolulu-based Northeast Asia Economic Forum (NEAEF) held in Toyama City, Japan, on October 25 and 26 (2007).

Following a performance by well-known Japanese violinist Yayoi Toda, opening remarks were delivered to the two hundred plus attendees by NEAEF Chairman Dr. Lee-Jay Cho, often thought of as the "godfather of NEA economic cooperation," Japanese Prime Minister Fukuda Yasuo, represented by former Japanese Foreign Minister and current member of the Japanese Diet (parliament) Nakayama Taro, former Governor of Hawaii George R. Ariyoshi, and a host of personages representing the governments and leaders of participating nations, Japan, South Korea, Russia, China, and Mongolia.

The two day conference consisted of presentations and panel discussions focused on achieving greater regional cooperation in environmental protection, energy conservation, and transportation integration among participating nations.

According to the Hokuriku Declaration, which was unanimously voted on at the end of the meeting, participants support "establishing a sustainable economy and society," while sharing a responsibility for controlling environmental degradation migrating across the region from one country to another.

A regional approach is to be pursued "to construct societies of low carbon use, recycling, and living with nature in safety and comfort."

As regional economic integration progresses, there must be more public-private cooperation. Exchanges of environmental information, assurances that personnel are prepared to enhance regional environmental governance, creation of new environmental technologies, and further development of industry and academia partnerships are needed to provide environmental protection. Financial incentives, in the form of foreign aid or low interest loans or grants, must be offered to preserve natural resources for future generations.

The supply of energy plays a crucial role in the further economic development and continued security of NEA. Demand is likely to expand as all NEA economies continue to grow. Therefore, "it is important to increase energy supply, and it is further important to improve energy efficiency." It was further agreed that, "promotion of nuclear energy with special attention to non-proliferation and other alternative energy resources would benefit NEA and the entire world."

To enhance the overall economic development of NEA requires further integration of regional transportation systems and added cooperation. For example, products could be shipped from Western Honshu (Japan's major economic and political center) ports to Korea to be loaded on to South Korean freight trains transiting North Korea and bound for the Russian Far East (RFE). Arriving there, those Japanese goods could then be loaded on the Trans-Siberian Railway for delivery to European markets resulting in lower shipping costs and quicker delivery than sea transport offers. The same is true for South Korean goods. Mongolia could also benefit by gaining access to the sea.

To realize a more regionally-integrated economy requires infrastructure improvements as well as the seeding of new industries. To promote regional financing, the meeting supported continued efforts to establish a Northeast Asian Development Bank.

Prior to the start of the October 25-26 meeting, the NEAEF conducted the Youth Leadership Training and Research Program (YLTRP) at the University of Toyama from October 14 to 27. A very impressive group of thirty-two highly intelligent young leaders from all participating countries including Taiwan were selected to join the YLTRP to support research, build personal networks, and plant the seed for future regional cooperation.

The 17th meeting will be held in Tianjin, China, which is a logical choice given the development of its waterfront Tianjin Binhai New Area (TBNA). The

TBNA will essentially be a huge free trade zone with a high concentration of manufacturing and research capability. This will provide for the economic growth of North, Northeast, and Northwest China that the Shenzhen and Zhuhai Free Trade Zones have done for Southern China. With its expanded port facilities to accommodate more trade, it will also offer economic benefit to all of NEA.

As interesting and productive as the meeting was, there were some obvious "omissions." Owing to difficulties in Japanese-North Korean bilateral relations, no Japanese visas were issued to North Korean representatives. North Korea is generally considered difficult to deal with, yet given its geographical location in the exact center of NEA it must be involved in all discussion about regional economic cooperation. This is especially important in coordinating rail links.

Save one graduate student from Taiwan studying in the U.S., no representative from Taiwan—an engine of economic growth with countless lessons in economic development to share and plentiful financial resources—was present.

The number of NEA organizations promoting regional economic cooperation is growing, yet there is a lack of synergy and a varying foci among them. Thus, the pace and scope of regional cooperation is reduced. In Southeast Asia, the Association of Southeast Asian Nations is the central organization successfully promoting regional economic interests. Without a similar organization in NEA, regional economic development will be hindered in maximizing its potential.

There was an apparent lack of big business interest in that no globally gauged corporation such as Japan's Toshiba, South Korea's Samsung, and China's Haier was present. It is difficult to understand how governments, think tanks, and academia can realize NEA regional economic cooperation without enthusiastic business involvement.

Nevertheless, regional economic cooperation is a long-term process that will one day create both greater mutual economic benefit and greater political cooperation in NEA.

Towards a Northeast Asia Bank for Cooperation and Development
Tianjin, China, November 9, 2008

Led by Chairman Dr. Lee-Jay Cho, a star-studded board with the services of former Governor George R. Ariyoshi, Nankai University, and co-sponsored with the Tianjin municipal government, the Honolulu-based Northeast Asia Economic Forum concluded a two-week series of events on October 29, 2008, to promote greater cooperation and financial integration in Northeast Asia (China, Japan, South Korea, Mongolia, and Russia) with linkages to the U.S.

Selected from a highly competitive pool of applicants, thirty-three finalists from China, Russia, Japan, South

Korea, Mongolia, and the U.S. participated in the Third Annual Young Leaders Training and Research Program in Regional Cooperation and Development or more simply called the Young Leaders' Program (YLP) organized by the NEAEF and hosted by Nankai University. The YLP was supported by a generous Freeman Foundation grant. All finalists were fluent in at least a second language, and represented a cross section of academic backgrounds and work experience.

During their two-week training period, the young leaders attended a wide variety of lectures presented by NEA countries concerning the organization's history as well as future economic development. In addition, they worked in collaborative groups on topics relevant to various aspects of regional economic growth, honing their intercultural skills in solving common problems with those from different cultures. Dr. Kovsh Andrey Vladimirovich, Lecturer in the Department of North American and Asia-Pacific Studies at Saint Petersburg State University in Russia, enjoyed the program so much last year that he participated again in 2008. He believes personal connections made during training are invaluable, and the networking will reap a flow of information and future career successes. His thoughts are echoed by Dr. Kim Nan-Young, Lecturer in Public Administration at Suwon University in Korea, who is pursuing post-doctoral research at China's Tsinghua University, and Sean Keith who is enrolled in the Master of Arts Program in International Policy Studies at the Monterey Institute of International Studies in California while simultaneously studying at Waseda University in Tokyo.

At the conclusion of the YLP, the young leaders joined in the 17th Annual Forum of the NEAEF from October 27 to October 28. The Forum was held in the Binhai New Area of Tianjin, which is being built up into a world class port facility. As a result, Binhai will help to stimulate NEA economies and regional integration.

The Forum agenda was divided into four sections: 1) Energy Cooperation; 2) Energy Conservation and Environment; 3) Transportation and Logistics Cooperation; and 4) Financial Cooperation and Development. Each section was addressed by a number of distinguished speakers from NEA nations as well as the U.S. Sharing similar goals with the NEAEF, Dr. Nataliya Yacheistova, Director of the United Nations Development Program Tumen Secretariat also participated in the Forum.

According to the Tianjin Binhai Declaration unanimously supported by attendees at the Forum's conclusion on October 29, Energy Cooperation in NEA acknowledges the challenges of responsibly ensuring the supply of energy in the region. NEA is not only the fastest economically growing region of the world, it is also the most economically volatile. To surmount the challenges, energy resources must be cooperatively developed and shared.

Energy Conservation and Environment in NEA requires more attention. As much as economic growth is sought in NEA, forum attendees agreed that rapid growth has exacted environmental damage adversely impacting the region's quality of life. Therefore, technology, government policies and programs plus market and regulatory incentives are needed to enhance efficient energy use, environmental conservation, and greater economic well being.

In regard to Transportation and Logistics Cooperation, attendees supported a multilateral approach to resolving problems pertaining to the transportation of resources between NEA nations. However, it was noted that a major hurdle to progress in this area is securing financing.

On the issue of Financial Cooperation and Development, the discussion focused on creating a strategy to reduce risk for international capital in investing in large scale inter-region projects. Significantly, attendees supported the creation of a regional bank that would be developed in a manner acceptable to NEA nations and help to expedite the flow of capital to development programs.

Consequently, the most significant event of the Forum was the attendees' adoption of the Tianjin Initiative, which gave exclusive attention to the establishment of a Northeast Asia Bank for Cooperation and Development (NEABCD). The bank would attract capital to be used in major cross-border projects to promote economic cooperation and development in a socially and environmentally acceptable manner that would promote regional economic integration. To enhance the achievement of such goals, and with strong support from the Tianjin Municipal Government, the NEA Financial

Cooperation Research Center was established at Nankai University to help expedite establishment of the NEABCD. Dr. Cho was appointed Visiting Chair Professor at Nankai University where he will periodically teach. Nankai is considered one of China's top three universities and is well known for the high quality of its economic analysis.

Despite the obvious successes of both the YLP and NEAEF, North Korea's absence was obvious. After all, the 1992 Forum was held in Pyongyang and North Korea is in the very center of NEA. As one of the most successful economies in NEA, Taiwan could contribute much to the Forum's success. Considering that both China and Taiwan are members of the World Trade Organization where Taiwan is considered a customs zone, rather than a nation, China should see Taiwan's participation in the Forum in the light of improving cross straits relations. Moreover, the U.S. should lend more support to NEA regional cooperation in that it promotes regional political stability, a key goal of U.S. policy in NEA, and offers business opportunities.

Chapter Two

CHINA

China of the 80s and Now
Honolulu, September 21, 2009

I first visited China in 1982, four years after China opened its doors to the world. In those days, China maintained a very uniform, unisex appearance. Nearly everyone wore dark blue, gray, or black high collared Zhongshan jackets with matching hats affixed with a red star. Such uniformity in dress made it difficult to distinguish between male and female. Today, Zhongshan jackets have largely been replaced by a wide variety of colorful wear. People are much more stylish and concerned about buying name brands.

The department stores of the 80s were dark, poorly stocked, and had inattentive service. Today, Chinese cities all boast modern, brightly lit, and well decorated department stores with a wide variety of goods from around the world. Customer service hot lines are readily available for shoppers with complaints.

Even in Beijing, there were far more bicycles in the streets than today. Most cars came from Russia or Japan. Today, the situation is reversed, with more cars than bicycles. Russian cars are not to be found. Instead, Audis, Buicks, Hyundais, and Volkswagens dominate the roadways.

China's infrastructure was very underdeveloped. Paved roads only ran from city centers to a few kilometers outside of city boundaries. Today, one can speed from the Northeast to the Southeast or from the East Coast to Gansu Province on a highway system that is just as good as any interstate highway in America. Airports are far more comfortable than in the past, and flights connecting every corner of country are more frequent.

At that time, university students only totaled one million. Today, there are millions. University graduates were assigned a work unit by the government; today, they find their own job. Studying in America was just beginning; at present, there are close to sixty thousand students from China in American institutions of higher learning.

All housing was owned by the government and assigned by work unit. Now people own their houses. Consequently, many attractive housing complexes have been built that look like they have been plucked from France or America and set down inside China.

Contemporary Chinese life is far more comfortable than in the 80s.

William E. Sharp, Jr.

China: The Old and New Faces of the Dragon
Honolulu, August 28, 2005

The beloved late Chinese Premier Chou Enlai once remarked to Tillman Durdin of the *New York Times* that China would not be a society of traffic jams, pollution, and materialism. Chou had little foresight of the wholesale changes that would soon transform Chinese life.

In the 1980s, those lucky enough to live in cities had a good chance of attending a high school. In the countryside, one might acquire a basic elementary education, if their commune could afford a school. Only one million students attended university. All aspects of the economy were controlled by the state, and college graduates were arbitrarily assigned to work units upon graduation.

Moving was strictly controlled by a special administrative tool, the "hukou" or family register which had to be signed by the police. Travel had to be related to work. Domestic and international moving and travel restrictions have been greatly reduced.

Work units controlled the distribution of quality of life benefits: grocery ration cards, health services, and housing were among the most important. All housing and land belonged to the state.

Bikes were the primary means of transportation. Private ownership of automobiles did not exist. Cars and drivers were assigned to high level party functionaries and to work units for official use. Travel by automobile from city to city was unpleasant since there were few good roads between cities. If one traveled, it would probably be by train. There was limited air service, but most passengers were functionaries or foreign tourists.

There were elections held at village level; however, self-criticism sessions where one had to confess deviance in political thinking were still mandatory. Political slogans, often written on red banners in white characters, adorned the streets of all cities and towns. Chinese addressed each other as "tongzhi" (comrade). Traveling overnight by train, one awoke in the early morning to a thunderous rendition of the national anthem, "March of the Volunteers," and the "Internationale." People were extremely careful in communicating their political views. Due to systematic control of "counterrevolutionary" literature, many Chinese born after 1949 were unable to read Chinese classics.

Obtaining membership in the Chinese Communist Party and being selected to serve in the People's Liberation Army (PLA) was very competitive. PLA service was a source of pride to families whose relatives had served, and it would likely lead to party membership, which translated into better jobs and better housing once discharged.

The unisex look prevailed and at times it was difficult to tell the sexes apart in that they all wore dark blue or grey, high collared jackets, baggy pants, and a cap with little red star. Little wonder, shopping in a dark, dank state department store was a depressing experience in that what little merchandise that was available was of low quality, comparatively expensive, and the service was blatantly poor.

This year, 3.5 million students will graduate from university. Educational opportunities are to be found at all levels in both state and private institutions, although the countryside still has some catching up to do. Now, they can freely choose where they wish to work. While the biggest key industries are still state dominated, many graduates start their own businesses.

Work unit influence in private life has vastly diminished. A growing number of people own their homes. Overnight, Chinese cities have become forests of gleaming new high rise condominiums, although the state still owns the land.

Bikes are still plentiful, but once car free city streets are jammed with autos emitting endless black clouds of pollution. Going intercity or to a distant countryside village is a fast and comfortable ride given China's nationwide "interstate system," boasting highways just as good as those in the U.S. On the freeway, it is common to see a family whizzing by in their Buick en route to a newly built mountain resort hotel where they can escape scalding hot weather.

Today, people talk of the need for more freedom and freely admit that there are problems with China's version of communism, but they also point out that, with the economic reforms, everyone now eats well. Billboards advertising the latest computer or fashion item have replaced publicly displayed political slogans. Traditional and popular music have supplanted revolutionary music and are played everywhere. A wide variety of information is readily available.

Far more trained lawyers are available, though at a price, and more trained judges are on the bench. An interesting program to train well-compensated jurors to participate in the decision of court cases on an equal basis with judges is being finalized.

Joining the party is not nearly as sought after and does not offer any special advantage. Like the U.S. military, the PLA has trouble meeting recruitment goals and has devised special enlistment and re-enlistment bonuses, stressing the educational benefits of military service.

Consumerism has ushered in an era of materialism. Men and women are both fashion conscious and shop in brightly lit, architecturally pleasing department stores with a wide variety of products sporting Chinese and foreign brand names. Clerks are polite, if also persistent, and notices are posted throughout department stores directing customers to complaint hotlines if there are any problems.

Adopting selective market mechanisms, Chinese life is far better. This does not mean that China has become a capitalist country. Most major industries still remain state industries. The omnipotence of the Chinese Communist Party is far less than it was; however, the party still holds ultimate power. Key decisions affecting millions are made by a few at the highest level of the party. However, the party is far more willing to investigate abuses of power and to bring about resolution. Ironically, while people feel free to criticize the party and some hope for a two-party system, they covet the stability the party underwrites. On summer vacation, they flock en masse to sites commemorating important revolutionary history such as Shaoshan Village, Mao's birthplace, and the Yanan Caves, the party headquarters during World War II.

Being further spurred on by the upcoming 2008 Beijing Olympics, China will continue to change, becoming even less recognizable to Chou.

China: Roaring Lion or Paper Tiger
Honolulu, January 1, 2006

Ever since the late Deng Xiaoping, father of China's contemporary economic development, took China off of the path to revolution in 1978 and put it on the highway of economic modernization, China has experienced phenomenal economic growth of 9.5% a year and sought to play a larger role in global economic and political affairs. While China's rise has been rapid, many observers have prematurely crowned China a "superpower."

Deng wanted China to recover from the economically ruinous Great Proletarian Cultural Revolution (1966-1976) and felt spurring Chinese on by promises of wealth that they would produce much faster. "Some will get rich before others," Deng said. He was entirely correct! In today's China, the widening gap between the relatively small number of those that have gotten rich and those that haven't is readily apparent. The chasm is particularly clear when comparing the lifestyle of residents in a handful of coastal cities with those living in the inland provinces. The Chinese public generally assumes that the nouveau riche has gained their new status through bribery, smuggling, cheating, deception, and all-purpose swindling. Given the omnipresence of the Chinese Communist Party in every facet of Chinese life, the complicity of party officials is widely recognized.

Land use issues provide the grist for much of the corruption in China. Despite agricultural liberalization, the state still owns all land. If farming is to be one's path to a better economic future, then one will have to successfully negotiate with local party officials to lease farmland for cultivation. Contracts in China don't carry the weight that they do in the U.S. If a local party official is persuaded that leased farmland can be better used as a site for a factory, power plant, shopping mall, or other enterprise, the party official will abuse their power by abrogating the contract and removing the farmer. Chinese law stipulates levels of compensation to be paid in such situations. However, the farmer normally receives a small percentage of the compensation, the bulk going into a party official's pocket or Hong Kong bank account.

A clear example of such took place on December 6, 2005, in the small fishing village of Dongzhou, located 125 miles northeast of Hong Kong in China's Guangdong Province. Farmers were being forced off the land in order for a coal generated power plant to be built there. The farmers felt that the compensation being offered was inadequate, and the power plant would harm air and water quality. For two months, they blocked the road into the construction site. Ultimately, the People's Armed Police, an arm of the People's Liberation Army, killed between ten and twenty protesters, resulting in the largest use of government violence to quell an uprising since the 1989 Tiananmen Incident.

Theoretically, the Chinese government has abolished agricultural taxes because local party officials purposely inflated the amount of tax that each farming family had to pay. After passing on the amount that Beijing mandated, they then kept the difference knowing that it was unlikely a farmer would go to court, given the collusion of local government and judicial officials plus the piecemeal organization of the Chinese judicial system. In Chinese, such a practice is known as "squeeze," and, unfortunately, has a long, deeply rooted history. It is only reasonable to assume that local officials will concoct some other system to supplement their income.

Like a wildly metastasizing cancer, corruption runs rampant. Chinese leaders realize that uncurbed corruption erodes popular public support. However, they are unable to stop it. To stop it requires using the party to clean up the party. A large-scale purge of corrupt party officials would turn large portions of the party against other parts of the organization. As a result, China would be cast into a period of internal turmoil and instability. Exactly what no Chinese wants.

Westerners and many Chinese contend that if China had popular elections to directly elect political leaders at all levels and an uncensored press, the corruption problem would disappear. However, Chinese President Hu Jintao has resisted any suggestion for wholesale political change. Instead, he has ordered a crack down on public dissent against corruption. In Hu's view, corruption will be solved through re-education of the perpetrators. Hu had better be right because according to the BBC and CNN, 74,000 protests, involving 3.7 million people broke out in China last year, largely due to land use and taxation issues. In 1994, there were only 10,000 protests. To counter further protests, the Chinese government announced the formation of elite police squads in thirty-six cities.

Before Deng announced his economic reforms, China was committed to the "iron rice bowl" policy of providing everyone with a job. As economically inefficient as it was, a factory that required a labor force of 125 to operate might have 250 workers. Hoping to rationalize the Chinese economy through privatization and limited foreign ownership, work forces were trimmed. The government promised new jobs in new enterprises; however, a lot of that promise has yet to be fulfilled. Chinese unemployment is estimated at 30%, with an underemployment rate to match. Such a phenomenon is particularly evident in Northeast China, a one time industrial center of China that is now considered the Chinese "Rust Belt."

Financial power is a key ingredient of superpower clout. Like Japan's banking system of the 90s and banks in Thailand, South Korea, and Indonesia, Chinese banks are poorly managed and have made billions of dollars of loans that will never be repaid. Loans have often been made based on political connections, rather than solid managerial principles or to keep faltering industries alive and workers employed. To bail itself out of this situation, China is selling interest in banks to foreign banks. Chinese stock markets in Shenzhen and Shanghai enjoy little trust among the Chinese and operate in a secretive, non-transparent way. As such, they are experiencing little vitality.

China's military power is growing, yet it is highly dependent on foreign technology. Cash strapped Russia depends on China to buy a large portion of its arms in order to maintain its defense industrial base. Nevertheless, Russian military planners realize that China poses a potential military threat owing to historic Chinese claims to large portions of the sparsely populated, natural resource rich Russian Far East. Thus, it does not sell China its most sophisticated military equipment. China has relentlessly urged the European Union to lift its arms ban, imposed after the Tiananmen Incident, reasoning that European radar and missiles will help them to better understand American weapons systems and tactics given the high level of cooperation between Europe and the U.S. Nor is it surprising that the Chinese have developed an extensive espionage system in the U.S. to covertly acquire military technological information about such important advances as the W-88, America's smallest nuclear warhead that can be launched from a submarine, and the means of making submarines operate silently.

Perception determines policy. Thus, it is imperative to maintain an objective view of both China's strengths and weaknesses.

The Tiananmen Incident – 20 Years On
Honolulu, September 5, 2009

Despite the spectacle of thousands of Chinese university students and workers amassing in Beijing's cavernous Tiananmen Square to protest for political liberalization and more effective measures against corruption, twenty years on the Chinese Communist Party (CCP) has done little to address both concerns.

The CCP's primary goal is to provide political stability which to China's detriment it has often lacked. Through the Leninist security apparatus, party control extends to every corner of Chinese society. As more and more private companies are formed, the party aggressively creates party branches in each. Universities demand particular scrutiny given that they are often the caldron of Chinese political protest. At the top, more and more members of the "Princeling Faction" (offspring of high level party elders) are gaining key positions since it is felt that they represent the most politically loyal segment of Chinese society.

With stability, the CCP has been able to focus on economic policies that have brought great economic development to China. Millions have been lifted out of poverty, and the country has witnessed a burgeoning middle class.

Pursuit of corruption is often a pre-text for bringing down a political opponent. Former Shanghai Party Secretary General Chen Liangyu engaged in many corrupt practices. However, he was ultimately brought down because of pointed differences with CCP General Secretary Hu Jintao.

Western inspired theories that the 80 to 100 million strong middle class will demand democracy have yet to be proven. Fearful that Western style parliamentary democracy will result in a loss of their newly gained wealth, China's middle class ranks among the staunchest supporters of the status quo.

Edited by leading China specialist Andrew Nathan and others, the recently published book *How East Asians View Democracy* argues that of all Asians, the Chinese are among the least interested in democracy.

Economic growth has cast China as a leading global economic player. At the April 2009 G-20 Conference in London, all eyes were clearly fixed on the country. Moreover, China's new global economic power has helped it to deflect criticism about undemocratic practices. Secretary of State Hillary Clinton's recent trip to Beijing was noticeably absent of criticism about China's lack of regard for human rights.

With more and more factories closing due to less demand abroad for Chinese products and unscrupulous land deals that fail to offer stipulated compensation to aggrieved parties, China has tens of thousands of demonstrations per year. In 2005, 87,000 were reported according to Ministry of Public Safety statistics. However, the focus is on economic justice, not democracy.

University professors, intellectuals, and an occasional party dissident might clamor for democracy, but to no avail. The recent Charter '08, based on the Czechoslovakian Charter '77 penned by dissidents in the former East Bloc country, was just such an example, from which it is hard to see any meaningful result in political liberalization. Moreover, key figures were incarcerated, stripped of CCP membership, and removed from the positions they held. Given government control over all published materials, university students have very little knowledge about the Tiananmen Incident, and are clearly more concerned about getting jobs and studying abroad.

While the post-Tiananmen era has seen a growing CCP interest in public consultation and in public polling to help guide policy, the only tangible growth of democratic spirit has been within the party itself. Such growth is the result of the growing influence of intra-party factions and the need to achieve consensus. Moreover, deeper discussion and cooperation are needed given the complexity of the problems that China now faces and the lack of a pre-eminent leader such as Mao Tse-tung or Deng Xiaoping.

But as for Western style democracy, one only has to recall the pointed words of Wu Bangguo, Chairman of the Standing Committee of the National People's Congress (which ranks him as the second highest leader in China) at the close of this year's session. Wu emphatically said there is no place in China for multi-party Western parliamentary democracy.

Will the Real China Please Stand Up
Honolulu, February 4, 2007

Starting in the 1950s and running in reincarnated form up until 2002, *To Tell the Truth* was a popular TV game show where panel members queried contestants in order to distinguish who really was the person introduced by the announcer. At the end of questioning, the real person had to stand up. Today, the world seems in as much of a quandary as the panelists often were, as they try to decipher the "real" China. Is it Marxist, Leninist, Stalinist, Maoist, or as many declare, capitalist just like the U.S.? Will the real China please stand up?

As created by Karl Marx and Friedrich Engels, Marxism interprets historical evolution as a reflection of society's productive powers. Marx and Engels are concerned with social classes, especially the "proletariat" or those who provide labor but do not own the means of production, and the "bourgeoisie" who own the means and employ the proletariat.

Marxists see society progressing in a linear fashion through four stages: feudalism, capitalism, socialism, and communism. Progression is energized by focusing attention on cultural and philosophical shortcomings that prevent advancement to the next stage. As each hurdle is overcome, a new synthesis of thought is created. Society will ultimately reach the stage of communism where each gives according to their ability, to each according to their need. There will be no need for a coercive state bureaucratic apparatus since everyone will be equal.

Contemporary China is generally free of the Marxist rhetoric that dominated in the past. There is no talk about class struggle or proceeding from one stage of history to the next. Not everyone has forgotten Marx; however, it is telling to note that his picture no longer accompanies Mao's over the entrance to the Forbidden City. Use of Marxist symbolism and jargon are primarily reserved for opening ceremonies at such formal events as the National Party Congress and National People's Congress.

Marxism-Leninism combines Marxism with Leninism, Vladimir Lenin's economic and political theories. Lenin emphasized the role of a communist party populated by professional revolutionaries and the dominant role of the state. Both the party and the state would act in the name of the proletariat, to guarantee their well being. Religion was to be strictly controlled since Lenin felt that it weakened the proletariat to the point that they were easily exploited. Lenin brooked no deviation and had no compulsion about using the coercive powers of the Cheka (forerunner of the KGB) to ensure compliance. Lenin introduced the New Economic Policy (NEP) in 1921, which allowed farmers to sell surplus production after a tax in kind was paid to the state. Agricultural production exploded.

"Stalinist" refers to a system of government that adheres to basic Marxist principles and the Leninist view of party and state preeminence. While Lenin employed coercion, Stalin employed terror and fear on a society wide scale. His purges of the 1930s and decimation of agricultural peasants underline the fact. His unpopular collectivization of agricultural no doubt contributed to further peasant unrest. Stalin ended Lenin's NEP and began the system of economic development based on five year plans, which featured greatly expanding heavy industry to strengthen the Soviet Union against the West. Thought of as a tyrant by many, others argue that without Stalin the Soviet Union might not have emerged victorious in World War II.

Stalin's rule was punctuated by unrelenting self-deification. China's post 1978 economic development sought to increase steel production, but to a much greater degree it got jump started by the promotion of light industry and consumer goods—something Russia still lacks. China's agricultural production has grown more in line with the Lenin's NEP than any aspect of Stalinism. Stalinist is a more appropriate description of North Korea where deification and terror play key roles in sustaining the leadership.

The essence of Maoism was formulated while Mao and the party were based in Yanan in northern Shaanxi Province during World War II. Mao understood the importance of economic development in making China a strong country, but he insisted that a fundamental transformation of Chinese people's political thought needed to first be achieved before economic goals could be pursued. Agricultural peasants represented the largest segment of Chinese society; therefore, Mao launched a peasant based revolution. Mao further wished to stamp out Confucian influence since he felt that Confucian decorum, how one should relate to another through a rigid system of relationships based on age and gender, made Chinese meek.

Strongly influenced by Marxism, Mao was a strong proponent of permanent revolution. Theoretically, he emphasized the need for "struggle" or the need for those with bad (anti-revolutionary) class backgrounds to confront the contradictions in their behavior, which prevented them from becoming more revolutionary. Mao's stature grew during the Yanan Period when he created "mass line," which forged strong bonds between the party and the peasants and required party officials to produce policies that the peasants wanted.

Because he is the one who created the New China, Mao is held in high esteem by large numbers of Chinese who regularly visit his hometown, mausoleum, and other places of revolutionary significance. Yet given his excesses during the Great Leap Forward (1958-1960) and Great Proletarian Cultural Revolution (1966-1976) and the millions who died or were killed because of him, Chinese do not wish a return to the past. Save for a few scattered groups such as the Maoist Nepalese guerrillas who seek to remodel Nepal in a Maoist fashion and who the Chinese government openly considers an embarrassment, Maoism lacks appeal.

William E. Sharp, Jr.

I cringe when I hear or read bold claims that China is capitalistic just like the U.S. Left in near economic ruin due to the excesses of the Cultural Revolution, the Chinese government sought economic incentives to restart agricultural production. Private plots allowed farmers to grow a certain amount of crops for the state and to sell their surplus on the free market. Clearly, the contemporary Chinese economy employs certain capitalistic conventions. It is mind boggling to listen to lectures by senior Chinese Communist Party officials extolling the virtues of market forces. Yes, some smaller Chinese businesses might well be completely privatized, but China is far from being morphed into a replica of the U.S.

State owned enterprises (SOEs) are the bedrock of the economy and while many have been partially privatized, the state still holds decisive, overriding control said Professor Yining Li, Dean Emeritus of the Guanhua School of Management at Beijing University, former member of the Chinese National People's Congress, and key author of Chinese privatization law, while recently visiting Hawaii Pacific University. Venture capitalism has contributed much to the U.S., but it is in a very early stage of development in China. The party is *the* pre-eminent institution in China whose tentacles reach everywhere. Thus, there is no American sense of laissez faire. The party's concern for maintaining pre-eminence impedes real judicial reform, wider use of elections, greater access to internet news, complete privatization of SOEs, or the creation of any other center of countervailing power.

So, will the *real* China please stand up?

Minxin Pei, Director of the China Program at the Carnegie Endowment for International Peace wrote in "The Dark Side of China's Rise" in the March/April 2006 issue of *Foreign Policy* that China might best be described as a "Neo-Leninist State." Pei's view is based on the strong role of the party guided state in controlling key sectors of the economy and blocking democratic development. When necessary, the state uses coercion to preserve its economic and political dominance. Somewhat reluctantly, Pei acknowledges that China has successfully used market forces to achieve great growth; however, he states that China's growth isn't as impressive as Japan's, South Korea's, or Taiwan's.

In a 2005 statement, World Bank President Paul Wolfowitz said, "China as we all know, has been the fastest growing economy in Asia for the past 20 years and has lifted more than 400 million people above U.S. $1 a day poverty levels in that time." Nevertheless, Pei maintains that the model has caused expenditures for health, education, housing, and old age pensions to be cut causing a particularly severe effect in the countryside; yet 30% of GDP goes to bail out banks that continue to make politically connected loans. Moreover, the regime has fostered cronyism and built its support base on the military, technocrats, foreign capital, professionals, and private entrepreneurs.

William E. Sharp, Jr.

Two Myths and One in the Making
Honolulu, December 14, 2008

The study of China is exciting because of its long history of great cultural achievements and often mysterious, spell bounding politics. After all, its influence has greatly affected many Asian neighbors through Buddhism, Confucianism, social revolution, Marxism, and a market economic approach to development embedded in authoritarianism. As a worldly Vietnamese once told me while I served as a soldier in Vietnam, "If you want to understand Asia, you first need to understand China."

As captivating as the study of China is, scholars, journalists, analysts, and others who daily consume themselves with deciphering China's every move constantly need to reassess their assumptions to seek balance in their interpretations and assessments. Unfortunately, there has always been a lot of starry-eyed hype about China from both the left and the right. While an undergraduate during the 1970s, "Mao worship" was in vogue. As more recent, balanced research shows, he was hardly a saint and is responsible for the deaths of millions. The American right tends to interpret China's epic economic transformation over the last thirty years in a way that validates, if not exaggerates, their own economic instincts.

In 1978, there was no private property in China. All commercial enterprises, banks, cars, etc., were owned by the state. There were no stock exchanges. After China began to accept loans from abroad, the economy began to grow until finally market economic mechanisms replaced command economy ones. As the economy began to sizzle at unprecedented growth rates, stock markets were created and many state owned enterprises began to be privatized.

All of this leads to MYTH #1: China is just as capitalistic as America. Or, economically they are just like us. However, in many "privatized" stock companies, the Chinese government is the largest stockholder, if not a significant minority stock holder. A prime example is the Haier Corporation. Often touted as China's premier corporation, it specializes in home appliances and seeks to mold itself as a player in the ever competitive global economy. China's commercial airlines are another case in point.

American style laissez faire has no philosophical or practical traction in the Middle Kingdom. Through the use of what we might call "administrative guidance," the government picks winners and losers by giving tax and financial incentives on one hand and policy and regulatory preferences on the other to certain companies. In this way, it is no different than Japan, South Korea, Taiwan, Germany, and France.

At the most, Chinese capitalism is "guided capitalism." Nevertheless, China has lifted 350 to 400 million people out of poverty.

MYTH #2: As China continues to develop economically, the growing middle class will demand a liberal democracy.

No! Pressure for democracy will not come to bear for some time. Chinese history records nearly five thousand years of history imbued with authoritarianism. When has China ever really shown broad based democratic instincts? When the Nationalists Chinese ruled China, they only held one election, and that was under U.S. pressure in 1947. In today's China, elections are only held at village level, after a very careful vetting of all candidates by the party.

China and other Asian countries are more concerned with political stability and economic growth than with democracy. They tend to see democracy as though it were a speeding car wildly out of control, squealing on two wheels around a corner at 90 miles per hour and not knowing whether it is going to safely make its way though the turn and land back on four wheels.

There is little fear of big government and often a need to feel dependent on some larger force. Many of the members of the new middle class fear that democracy would somehow result in legislation that would diminish their newly gained wealth.

Democracy is built on institutions that ultimately have the power to check the power of other institutions. China has only one such institution of any significance: the Chinese Communist Party. The legal system, for example, is getting better but is designed primarily to protect the state. Like everything else, it is subservient to the party. Mass media is carefully controlled. Nevertheless, China's national leadership is much more sensitive to opinion polls than it has been.

MYTH # 3 in the making: China is strongly devoted to non-interference in the internal affairs of other countries.

After the establishment of the People's Republic of China in 1949, China largely cut itself off from the outside world, and most countries still recognized the Republic of China government on Taiwan as the government of China. However, in its earliest international dealings in the mid-1950s, which took place with India, the Five Principles of Peaceful Co-Existence were signed and promulgated by both countries. From these principles, China adopted the notion of non-interference in the internal affairs of other countries as a basic pillar of its foreign policy.

China's foreign policy is largely based on securing access to natural resources. In Sudan, China has invested over $10 billion in the energy industry and stationed 4,000 People's Liberation Army soldiers to guard its investment. What if the Sudanese were to suddenly announce nationalization of all oil assets in the country? The *International Business Daily* alleged, "China is the unindicted co-conspirator in Khartoum's genocidal campaign" in Darfur. China provides the Sudanese government with weapons, as well as diplomatic support at the UN, where it can use its Security Council veto to blunt any criticisms. Similarly, China supports the Myanmar (Burmese) junta, politically and with economic aid and arms. In return, Myanmar affords China strategic access via the sea to the Middle Eastern oilfields. Myanmar's proximity to China's rival, India, and the provision of a gateway to other natural resources makes Myanmar triply important. China has built four naval bases in the country where Chinese naval engineers have been spotted wearing civilian clothes. For some time, China has been involved in attempting to dilute the historic Vietnamese influence in Laos by vigorously wooing the country to the point that a growing number of Laotians question China's influence on the government.

It might have borrowed elements of American capitalism; however, China has created its own model of economic development that holds no foreseeable role for democracy. For some countries, it's an enviable model. The challenge for America is to reinvigorate its economy and ever build its democracy in a way that buoys America's soft power and global image.

"Beijing Speak"
Honolulu, October 8, 2006

Beijing's political lexicon is populated with a wide variety of political slogans and mottos (biaoyukouhao) typical of a particular era and leadership style. Slogans and mottos of this sort are quick and easy to read and can be found everywhere: on signboards, bulletin boards, newspapers, and television. Reminiscent of Orwell's "newspeak," such language might be called "Beijing Speak."

On both sides of the huge portrait of Mao Tse-tung suspended over the entrance to Beijing's Forbidden City where Mao proclaimed the establishment of the People's Republic of China in 1949 are two prominent slogans of the time: "Long Live the People's Republic of China" (Zhonghua Renmin Gongheguo Wansui) and "Long Live the Great Unity of People Throughout the World" (Shijie Renmin Da Tuanjie Wansui). In 1952, the "Three Antis" (Sanfan) focused on eliminating corruption, stifling bureaucracy, waste, and the "Five Antis" (Wufan) targeted bribery, tax evasion, theft of state property, theft of economic information, and shoddy workmanship.

Starting in 1966, the Cultural Revolution spawned a wide variety of new political slogans. The best known was "To Rebel is Justified" (Zaofanyouli), which sought to justify attacks on the CCP and all forms of authority, including parents. Beginning in 1977, Deng Xiaoping eagerly set China on a new economic path, free of the socialist blinders that had held China's economy back. "Seek truth from facts" (Shishiqiushi) encouraged the Chinese public to welcome economic growth, even if it meant departing from orthodox Marxist notions of economic development and adopting some aspects of capitalism. "White cat, black cat as long as it catches the mouse is what makes a good cat" (Buguan heimao baimao neng zhuadao laoshu jiushi haomao). In other words, it is the end result, not the means that really matters.

Jiang Zemin, 80, served as President of China, General Secretary of the CCP, and Chairman of the Central Military Commission during the period of 1993 to 2004. During his tenure, China experienced phenomenal 8% annual growth in its Gross Domestic Product (GDP) aggressively shepherded over by Premier Zhu Rongji, who many dubbed "China's economics czar." With Jiang and Zhu at the helm, China's economy took on global significance, was finally admitted to the World Trade Organization, and was selected as the 2008 Summer Olympics site. Clearly, Jiang realized the growing power of the global economy and wanted to ensure a permanent position for China.

To do so, Jiang promulgated his *Three Represents* (sangedaibiao) theory. In his speech at the 16th Party Congress in 2002, Jiang stated:

> Reviewing the course of struggle and the basic experience over the past 80 years and looking ahead to the arduous tasks and bright future in the new century, our Party should continue to stand in the forefront of the times and lead the people in marching toward victory. In a word, the Party must always represent the requirements of the development of China's advanced productive forces, the orientation of the development of China's advanced culture, and the fundamental interests of the overwhelming majority of the people in China.

Interpretations vary as to the exact meaning of individual parts of the Three Represents. What is clear is that Jiang used his theory to justify entry of highly successful, new, private business people into the party to help China's economy keep growing.

National leaders in any system ultimately want to create a legacy; Jiang is no exception. Despite grumbling within the party about the focus on businessmen in view of China's widening income gap, Jiang's theory was incorporated into the CCP and Chinese State Constitutions. Moreover, Jiang attempted to use his theory to promote himself as an equal to Mao and Deng, which in most Chinese and foreign analysts' eyes was a stretch. After all, Mao created the New China, and Deng put it on the road to economic prosperity. Jiang's leadership is not without merit; however, he advanced Deng's vision rather than having created any fundamental change in direction. Mao and Deng are held in high esteem; Jiang gets mixed reviews.

While Jiang might be considered more of a coastal elitist, his successor Hu Jintao, 64, is identified with inland China and the "laobaixing" (everyday people). Hu and Premier Wen Jiabao came to power in March 2003 in the wake of Jiang's and Zhu's phenomenal economic growth and the resulting socioeconomic problems that came with it, for example, growing economic gaps between the haves and have nots throughout Chinese society; regional economic disparity between the coastal and inland provinces; high unemployment and underemployment abetted by economic privatization; a faltering health care system; and rapacious corruption at all levels.

At the March 2006 National People's Congress, Hu and Wen put forth proposals to address economic problems and to improve the availability of health services. Moreover, they have sought to slow down the overheating economy and to curb inflation. Western countries are not free of corruption but keep it under control through a free press, independent judiciary, fair elections, and the presence of countervailing political forces. In the main, China lacks these conventions. Given the omnipotent power of the CCP, it is generally accepted that corruption cannot exist without the connivance of the party or individual party members. Corruption has a very definite corrosive effect on political stability and popular credibility. In other words, it can channel the benefits of economic progress to those with a special connection and stymie economic growth, the only reason that many continue to support the party.

It is clear from Hu's speeches that he realizes corruption is a major problem. It is even clearer that he has no intention of employing any Western type convention to combat it. Instead, the former head of the Central Party School advocates education. As such, on March 4, he announced his *Socialist Concept of Honor and Disgrace—Eight Do's and Eight Don't's* (shehuizhuyi rongruguan—barongbachi) which is a moral code for party members and non-party members to learn, to practice, and to live by:

1. Love the motherland, don't harm it
2. Serve, don't disserve the people
3. Uphold science, don't be ignorant and unenlightened
4. Work hard, don't be lazy

5. Be united and help each other, don't benefit at the expense of others
6. Be honest, not profit mongering
7. Be disciplined and law-abiding, not chaotic and lawless
8. Know plain living and hard struggle, do not wallow in luxuries

China has a history of key political leaders seeking to prolong their influence as long as possible. In 2004, Jiang resigned the Chairmanship of the Central Military Commission (CMC). Having earlier resigned his positions as General Secretary of the CPP and President of the People's Republic of China, Jiang was lauded for quietly and peacefully going into full retirement; however, conjecture ensued that Hu's party supporters pressured Jiang to resign from the CMC far before his term was to expire in 2007. In August of this year, Jiang resurfaced on the national stage when two books that he authored went on sale. One book is chocked full of pictures taken during his many foreign visits as Chinese President; the other is a three-volume set, *Selected Works of Jiang Zemin.*

Given the influence of the "Shanghai Clique," a group of leaders that Jiang appointed to key positions before retiring, it is noteworthy that Jiang should reappear at this time. There is an ongoing struggle for influence between Jiang and Hu. Jiang wanted Zeng Qinghong, rather than Hu, to have succeeded him. Moreover, Jiang's Shanghai Clique and Hu's loyalists have policy differences.

Although Hu's and Wen's term runs until 2012, Hu is obviously concerned that Jiang might be starting to hatch a scheme to influence the selection of Shanghai Clique members as the next generation of leadership at the upcoming 17th Communist Party Congress to be held in late 2007. The consequences for Hu would be difficulty in consolidating his leadership.

Hu has been acting like a velvet hammer. His recent speeches have played up Jiang's Three Represents in an obvious attempt to appease him. On the other hand, Chen Liangyu, First Secretary of the Shanghai CPP and a leading Shanghai Clique member was arrested and removed from power on September 25 of this year. Chen allegedly peddled his influence, gave special favors to family members, protected staff involved in illegal activities, and siphoned off money from Shanghai's social security fund. It is unfortunate that when a high level Chinese leader is arrested and/or removed from power, political reasons can be the motivating factor. Thus, it is not surprising the BBC reported that many China analysts have concluded the real reason for Chen's demise is Hu's attempt to strengthen his position before the party congress.

Fanning Chinese Nationalistic Pride
Honolulu, December 10, 2006

Super engineering and architectural projects are

worn as a badge of honor and pride in Chinese history, for example, the 3,000 mile plus long Great Wall, which defends China against its Northern enemies and the Grand Canal connecting Central China with Northern China. Architectural standouts include the Forbidden City and the growing number of skyscrapers in Beijing and Shanghai. As a whole, such projects are a source of great nationalistic pride.

The first major engineering achievement of the post-1949 Chinese government was the Nanjing Bridge. There had never been any bridge running across the Yangtze River at Nanjing. In 1958, Chinese authorities requested Soviet engineers working in China to study the feasibility of building such. The Soviets had designed and planned a span but soon rolled their plans up and took them home in the wake of the Sino-Soviet split.

In 1960, Chairman Mao Tse-tung directed Chinese engineers to design and build the Nanjing Bridge. The task was especially challenging given Chinese engineers lack of relevant experience, the Yangtze's fast currents and the rapidly rising and falling tides. Nevertheless, work on the bridge commenced in 1960. Upon completion in 1968, Chinese engineers had created a bridge 4 miles long and 525 feet wide that had two decks for vehicular traffic and trains.

The bridge contributed significantly to Chinese self-esteem and self-reliance. It has long been an automatically included stop for both foreign and domestic tour groups visiting Nanjing. In practical terms, the bridge facilitated train travel and sped the movement of goods resulting in greater economic benefit for both producers and consumers. The bridge also enabled more rapid deployment of troops and weaponry.

Located on the Yangtze River close to Chongjing in Western China, Sun Yat-sen's 1919 dream was finally realized in a May 20 topping-off party. The Three Gorges Dam is the largest dam in the world standing 544 feet high and covering 1.4 miles in length, making it five times the size of the Hoover Dam. The price tag is reported at $25.2 billion.

In April 1992, former Premier Li Peng vigorously promoted the dam in the National People's Congress despite obstreperous objection from one-third of the representatives in the normally docile body. Trained as a hydroelectric engineer and having held many important positions dealing with power generation, Li clearly saw the need for added power. Considered underdeveloped, Western China's living standard and economy will benefit from added power. The dam will provide 2% of national energy needs by 2010. In other words, the dam produces 18,200 megawatts of power, or enough power to supply a city four times the size of Los Angeles. Moreover, the Yangtze River's incessant overflowing has claimed over 300,000 lives during the last century. The dam should prevent overflowing.

While the benefits are clear, so are the costs. To create the dam, 2 cities, 11 counties, and 116 towns, and 1,200 villages had to be flooded, taking with them many cultural and architectural relics. With no place to live, 1.3 million villagers had to be relocated and 172,000 still have to be moved. The government appropriated $4.82 billion or $375 per person, for use in an area where incomes are as low as $180 a year, to compensate and resettle residents of communities that are now under water. However, many residents are unsatisfied, claiming that the party cadre did not pay them what they were due, pocketing the difference. A journalist turned activist Dai Qing ended up serving ten months in a maximum security jail after publishing her book, *Yangtze! Yangtze!* The book depicted the dam as a waste of money and an environmental disaster. Environmentalists and scientists contend that the reservoir behind the dam will evolve into a huge cesspool that will contaminate water for the 30 million residents in the greater Chongqing area. Nevertheless, the Three Gorges project represents an achievement on the scale of the Panama Canal.

On July 1, 2006, the Chinghai-Tibet Railway (CTR) was officially opened by President Hu Jintao, enabling travel from Golmud in Chinghai Province to Lhasa in the Tibet Autonomous Region. The 708 mile long railway is the first to connect Tibet with China proper and enables rail travel from Beijing to Lhasa, a distance of 2,500 miles taking 48 hours to cover.

Completion of the CTR has set new engineering and technical world records, for instance, the construction of the world's highest rail tracks at 16,640 feet altitude, which traverse the Tanggula Pass and the Fenghuoshan Tunnel, the world's highest rail tunnel at 14,700 feet above sea level. Together they express the seriousness of Chinese engineering. Of the Golmud to Lhasa stretch,

80% is built at an altitude greater than 12,000 feet, over half is on permafrost, and there are 675 bridges. The permafrost is not always so permanent, resulting in the ground becoming muddy. Chinese engineers had to modify their construction plans and create a system circulating liquid nitrogen and nitrogen gas into the ground to keep it frozen.

No doubt the railway will speed the delivery of freight to and from Tibet. A Chinese Academy of Social Sciences study concluded that by 2010, three-fourths of all freight to and from Tibet will be transported by rail. While the government pitches the economic growth that will follow, Tibetans see these benefits largely accruing to Han Chinese. Critics see the railway more as a tool to exercise greater control over Tibet, to protect Chinese defense concerns, and to facilitate extraction of natural resources. Additional concern is expressed over the negative impact on the environment and animal life.

Reflecting Chinese superstitious belief that the number "8" brings good luck and prosperity, the Beijing Summer 2008 Games commenced on 8/8/2008 at 8:08 and closed on 8/24/2008. China's hosting of the games symbolized the country's growing global economic and political stature, just like the Tokyo Olympics of 1964 did for Japan. Perhaps this explains China's selection of "The Same World, the Same Dream" as the game's motto.

Hosting an Olympics requires first rate logistical, technological, and managerial skill. Working in a very methodical fashion, China is unlikely to evince the worry that Athens did when many feared that it would be unable to successfully host the 2004 Olympics. Already 300,000 houses have been demolished to make room for the 36 stadiums, 59 training centers, convention center, Olympic Village, Olympic Aquatic Park, and the Wukesong Cultural and Sports Center.

Closely covered by media throughout the world, Olympics not only serve as a global arena for athletic events, they also are a global stage for political protest. Chinese authorities are already concerned about activity of the Students for Free Tibet and other supporters of Tibet Independence. Also politically sensitive is how Taiwan should participate, if it participates at all. Will the Mainland Chinese insist that Taiwan participate as "Chinese Taipei?" If so, will Taiwan accept, or just stay home?

China's celebrated engineering and architectural projects show China's growing technical and managerial skills, as well as the party's ability to deliver results that clearly build nationalistic pride while taking, if only momentarily, people's attention off of the country's rampant corruption.

China's 10th NPC: Putting All Under Heaven in Order
Honolulu, April 8, 2007

Of great concern to most was the 17.8% increase in military expenditure introduced at the twelve-day National People's Congress beginning March 16, 2007.

As important as the increase was to foreign observers, the real focus of the NPC was on righting domestic social inequities and injustice. After all, both Chinese Communist Party General Secretary Hu Jintao's and Premier Wen Jiabao's speeches are laden with concern for creating a "harmonious society" (hexieshehui) or having all sectors of society smoothly functioning together, effecting a "reasonably comfortable society" (xiaokangshehui) that is predominately middle class. Unattended quality of life issues threaten China's political stability. Understanding such domestic issues might well be a better gauge of China's power equation than simple fixation on military power, as important as it is.

The NPC is China's parliament and meets annually in Beijing's Great Hall of the People for the 3,000 delegates to pass legislation. Normally considered a docile instrument—largely absent of the spirited debate for which other parliaments are known—the NPC is a rubber stamp rendering the proceedings a big yawn. However, recent sessions suggest the beginning of a break with the past as more delegates begin to represent their constituency's interest.

Since China introduced its economic reforms in 1978, the economy has grown at an annual average break neck speed in excess of 9.5%. All of which sounds good but which has also fueled inflation and opportunities for corruption. To address both problems, Wen announced that China would hold economic growth this year to 8%. However, he set the same goal last year only to see the economy grow at 10.7%.

China's income gap is crucially important to the leadership. According to Chinese government statistics reported in the Xinhuanet, the Gini co-efficient for China is quickly approaching 0.5, the critical point having been 0.4. The wealthiest 10% of the population control over 40% of assets; the poorest 10% only control 2% of assets. The income gap can also be seen in the income disparity between urban and rural residents and between regions. According to the Economist Intelligence Unit, urban incomes were 3.2 times larger than rural incomes in 2005. Regionally, coastal China is generally considered well off while Qinghai and Gansu Provinces in the West are considered poor and underdeveloped.

Not only are there gaps in income and wealth, there are additional gaps in educational opportunities offered in more developed, urban areas and less fortunate locales. In 2007, Wen promised to increase investment in education by 42% and to abolish tuition in the countryside, guaranteeing nine years of free education. In addition, the 2007 budget increases expenditures for medical care by 87%.

Extortionate rural taxation and unprincipled termination of rural land leases have greatly contributed to violent countryside demonstrations, some requiring lethal force to quell, that have grown from 58,000 in 2003 to 87,000 in 2005, according to Ministry of Public Safety statistics.

Tax exploitation is endemic in the Chinese countryside. Local officials receive a mandate from higher level officials to generate a certain amount of tax revenue and pass it upwards. They then bloat the figure, causing many economically marginal families to pay more than they can manage, and then skim the inflated part off for their own benefit. As Hu and Wen well know, the fall of dynasties throughout Chinese history has largely been caused by excessive taxation of agricultural peasants. Addressing the NPC, Wen reminded delegates that in 2006, Hu and Wen had ended the 2,600 year tradition of agricultural peasants paying taxes.

All rural land in China is owned by the state and leased to farmers. As has happened so often in recent years, a developer appears who wants to build a shopping mall or factory. They cultivate the local party secretary and persuade him or her to break the lease on the land of interest. Of course, they reward the secretary for their assistance who also benefits by skimming off a certain percentage of government supplied compensation for the displaced land tenants. Being abruptly yanked off of the land and not receiving fair compensation has also fuelled protest. The practice has grown like an uncontrollably spreading forest fire, driven by a wild wind. To prevent further exploitation and preserve stability, the NPC agreed to eliminate the regulation allowing the state to requisition land for development once leased.

Urban land is also owned by the state. In China's ongoing real estate boom, many middle class families have bought houses, condominiums, and other forms of housing and wanted to be assured that the land would not be pulled out from underneath them. Realizing the importance of the middle class to China's continued economic growth, it was expected that urban leases would be automatically lengthened.

The most contentious bill before the NPC was the Property Law of the People's Republic of China (wuquanfa). First discussed fourteen years ago and tabled without a vote at last year's NPC, the property law could only be passed this year after vigorous lobbying before the NPC convened. Private businesses contribute 65% of China's GDP and pay 70% of the taxes. Thus, the government has felt an increasing need to assure private business owners, the middle class, and other pillars of the burgeoning economy that their private property is protected. Contrarily, remnant Marxists hold another view. Han Deqiang, Beijing University of Aeronautics and Astronautics economist said, "The property law basically takes all the illegally gotten income and legalizes it. It's too liberal. It is too right wing. This is a step back to the laissez faire ideas of the 18th Century." Others opined the socialist fundamentals upon which the New China was founded would be violated.

It is questionable how well enforced and administered these new laws and reforms will be. "There is a distinction between law and actual reality," said Han Xu, a Chinese Academy of Social Sciences political scientist. Moreover, they put more power in the hands of the central government at the loss of provincial and local government cadres' power and opportunity for corruption, according to Bill O'Grady, Chief Global Strategist for A.G. Edwards. Provincial and local officials, throughout

Chinese history, have scuttled central government initiatives.

Hu definitely needs to show progress by September 23 when the 17th National Party Congress convenes in order to consolidate his leadership, enabling him to place more of those directly allied to him in key positions and to influence the make-up of China's next generation of leadership.

Shiqida: 17th National Party Congress
Honolulu, September 9, 2007

Before China opened to the world in 1978, China-watching was centered in Hong Kong. China-watchers seemed dedicated to examining every bit of information that slowly dripped out of China. For example, they read read transcripts of radio broadcasts, newspapers, escapee and defector interviews, as well as Hong Kong residents allowed over the border to visit relatives. China-watching was a guessing game to some degree.

Clearly, contemporary China is still not as transparent as Westerners would like. Nevertheless, acquiring Chinese data has gotten a lot easier with newspapers, academic journal articles, TV documentaries, and books constantly being churned out and flowing freely to other countries. "Baidu," China's equivalent of Google, facilitates speedy investigation of Chinese affairs. Foreign academicians can do research in China and representatives of Chinese state sponsored think tanks and retired government officials participate in international forums open to the public.

Yet, complete secrecy still prevails when it comes to the National Party Congress (NPC). In fact, while it was generally felt that the NPC would convene in October, 2007, the exact date was either not made public because of internal political jockeying or remained known to only a very, very small number of people at the summit of the Chinese Communist Party who wish to keep the date secret to thwart public demonstrations. The NPC, with its 2,200 delegates theoretically selected by grassroots party organizations, meets every five years to review the direction the party is going and to appoint top Chinese leaders to both the Politburo Standing Committee (PSC) and the full Politburo. When the NPC is not in session, its work is carried out by the Central Committee whose size varies from two to three hundred members representing the party, state, and military. The PSC and Politburo are the very most important decision making bodies in China with the smaller PSC having more clout than the Politburo. The size of the PSC varies, but generally runs from five to nine members while the Politburo might have nineteen to twenty five members. There are also a limited number of alternate members appointed to each body.

During the first (1949-1976) and second generations (1976-1997) of political leadership after the establishment of the People's Republic of China in 1949, strong figures like Mao Tse-tung and Deng Xiaoping exercised absolute control in the PSC and could pretty much rule China as they saw fit. Starting with the third generation (1989-2002) of leadership, led by Jiang Zemin, Chinese leaders have been better educated; however, they have lacked the political and revolutionary pedigree of their predecessors. Consequently, they have had to rely on negotiation and persuasion to win support from other PSC and Politburo members.

Moreover, as China became more involved with the world and China's economy continued to rapidly grow, decisions have become too challenging for any one person to make. Groups representing divergent party, ministry, regional, political, economic, and industrial demands have surfaced within China rendering decision making even more complex, requiring an ever increasing array of leadership skills, and a growing need to be sensitive to public opinion.

There is little doubt that both key fourth generation leaders, Hu Jintao, General Secretary of the Chinese Communist Party, and Wen Jiabao, Premier of the People's Republic of China, will be reconfirmed for another five-year term in those offices and on the PSC. Just who else will join them on the PSC is open to question, although it seems Wu Banguo, Chairman of the National People's Congress (China's parliament) Standing Committee, and a member of the "Shanghai Clique" or those remaining loyal to Jiang, will continue on the PSC, according to the August 2007 edition of the Hong Kong-based *Dongxiang (Trend) Magazine*. Due to the growing complexity of Chinese society and the historic difficulty in governing such a highly populated large area, there's reason to believe that the new PSC and Politburo will represent a greater balance of interests.

Creating that balance is the greatest challenge facing Hu Jintao's consolidation of power at the NPC. Hu's predecessor, Jiang Zemin focused his energies on building the economy of China's East Coast. To do so, he appointed those loyal to him to the PSC, Politburo, and as party provincial first secretaries and governors. Hu and Wen have tried to slow China's economic growth while spreading China's wealth more evenly by developing poorer Western China, pumping new economic life into Northeastern China, and fashioning themselves as the guardians of those economically left behind. Hu and his supporters are known as the "Communist Youth League of China Faction" since they were all politically reared during service with the Communist Youth League (CYL). They feel they would be more successful if the Shanghai Clique were replaced by those who share Hu's views. Yet, the Shanghai Clique still has influence and rarely in Chinese history have those with power easily stepped aside. Compounding the complications in creating a new balance is the animosity existing between Jiang and Hu that emerged at the end of the 16th NPC in 2002. Hu outmaneuvered Jiang by amassing more support in his campaign to become General Secretary. Jiang had supported Zeng Qinghong, a very loyal longtime protégé, who was invaluable to Jiang during the pinnacle of his political career because of his familiarity with the inner workings of the CCP at the highest levels.

In July, 2007, during the lead-up to the NPC, Hu incarcerated and expelled Shanghai First Secretary Chen Liangyu from the CCP for using Shanghai social security funds to speculate in real estate. Chen refused to go along with national economic policies aimed at taming the overheated economy. Hu might have felt that Chen's ouster would disband the Shanghai Clique and permanently dissipate any power Jiang might still have. It hasn't.

Once the formula for creating the balance is achieved, discussion can focus on who will succeed Hu and Wen at the 18th NPC in 2012. Likely key fifth generation leaders could include Xi Jinping, a highly successful Governor of Fujian Province. He also served as First Secretary of Fujian and Zhejiang Provinces. In September, he was appointed as Party First Secretary of Shanghai. Another contender, Li Keqiang, won central government kudos for reforming the moribund state owned enterprise dominated economy in Liaoning Province where he serves as First Secretary. Li also served as the Governor of Henan Province and holds a doctorate in economics from Bejing University. Bo Xilai, another former Governor of Liaoning Province and currently a highly successful national Minister of Commerce, is another possible candidate for future leadership. Both Xi and Bo's credentials are further burnished because their fathers played key roles in the founding of the PRC. As such, they are known as members of the "Princeling Faction" along with other party members who derive benefit from their fathers' contributions to China. Hu is reported to believe that only those with such strong familial connections to the CCP will make great national leaders. Yet, Zeng's father also played an important role in the founding of New China, and it is anyone's guess whether he will retain his PSC seat to mollify Jiang and out of deference to his father or lose it because of his connection to Jiang.

Only after the NPC has determined who will sit on the PSC and Politburo, and established who will succeed Hu and Wen, can possible reform and vital Chinese concerns be fully addressed. Some of these concerns include curbing corruption, beefing up the legal system, expanding intraparty democracy by giving the CCP more real power, ensuring that the 2008 Olympics lives up to expectations, slowing economic growth, managing relations with America, and maintaining peace in the Taiwan Strait.

And just when will we know the NPC will start? Based on previous NPCs, it will probably begin a few days after busloads of police arrive at the Great Hall of the People, across from Tiananmen Square, and start cordoning off the area.

Protecting 8 – "Bao Ba"
Honolulu, January 11, 2009

Despite having navigated an economy that has grown from a worldwide GDP of 1.8% in 1978 to 6% today and sustained an average economic growth rate of nearly 10% for thirty years, the Chinese economy is encountering daunting challenges. How well China manages those challenges and meets socio-economic commitments will clearly impact every Chinese person's life. If not managed well, civil unrest leading to political instability will evolve.

For many Chinese and international observers, China's economic situation comes as a surprise, if not a shock given China's effusive national Olympic pride and celebration of thirty years of economic reform.

With a budget surplus that already totaled $147 billion at the end of August and included nearly $2 trillion in foreign reserves, there was growing hope that the Chinese economy would pull the world out of economic malaise. On the contrary, Chinese officials' actions signaled that the best way China could help the world was to first help itself.

Questions first began to surface about China's economic wherewithal after last spring's earthquakes in Southwest China where 68,000 perished and billions of dollars in reconstruction was required. The towering need for assistance in the Southwest came on top of Chinese leaders' commitment to improve the rural quality of life.

China's phenomenal economic success has been the result of what economists call the "East Asia Economic Model" (EAEM). This is essentially the same mode of economic development that has worked so well for Japan, South Korea, and Taiwan. The EAEM is export driven, dependent on cheap labor, and seeks to hold exchange rates artificially low.

One only has to see the spate of Chinese products on store shelves throughout the world to realize the model's success. However, the global economic slow-down and U.S. recession reduced Chinese exports in November 2008 by 2% over the November 2007 total. Guangdong Province, a key Chinese export hub responsible for 12% of China's 2007 GDP by the end of November 2008 reported that its growth contracted by one-third.

Overall, domestic and foreign investment is not as forthcoming. Even before the slowdown, the central government began to address demands of factory workers by enforcing labor legislation to improve working conditions. Particularly galling to some employers has been government insistence on forming labor unions and Chinese Communist Party cells within enterprises. To many, India, Vietnam, and other investment destinations offer better profit making opportunities.

Sloganeering plays an important role in Chinese politics. Its latest slogan, "bao ba" or maintaining a growth rate of 8% permeates a lot of contemporary Chinese economic thinking. China claims that it needs to maintain an annual growth rate of 8% to create the 7 million jobs it annually needs to create to stem the growing unemployment rate that officially stands at 4.5%, but is generally thought to be much higher. The World Bank estimates economic growth will be 7.5% while the International Monetary Fund limits growth to 5%.

After years of U.S. pressure, the Chinese allowed the

yuan to appreciate. To date, it has appreciated by 20%. Some Chinese economists are promoting the view that the yuan should depreciate to stimulate exports. The view has gained some traction given Guangdong's experience. Depreciating the yuan at this point would bring swift American rebuke given the long-term U.S. effort to encourage China to allow the yuan to appreciate. In other words, it would reverse what many observers see as a promising trend: the reduction of China's $256 billion trade surplus with the U.S. in 2007 to $223 billion in 2008.

Similar to other countries, China launched a stimulus package worth $586 billion dedicated to infrastructure improvements such as roads, bridges, railways, harbors, rural housing, environmental protection,and earthquake-proofing. However, many question the actual amount claiming that it includes monies already budgeted in the 2006-2010 five-year plan. Beijing was also trying to fund the package with local government and private business resources. Another school of thought argues that to do what China says it wants to achieve, a stimulus package of $1.2 trillion is actually needed.

To make up for a shortfall in exports, support for stimulating domestic demand has grown. However, the average Chinese household savings of 4,000 yuan ($588) does not offer much reason to hope the Chinese will go on a shopping frenzy. Realizing the economic downturn, Chinese families prudently want to hold on to their savings in order to pay educational expenses, medical bills, and to meet other unknown expenses. Actually, this strategy seems to offer even less hope than might be expected in that China has periodically tried unsuccessfully to stimulate domestic demand in order to deflect international criticism of China's trading successes. Owing to a lack of reliable social services, people have been impelled to save rather than to spend. Tax reductions will also likely have little effect for the same reasons.

Party officials advocated a reduction in interest rates while the People's Bank of China (PBOC) wanted to continue fighting inflation. Keeping in mind the strength of China's budget surplus, the PBOC finally reduced its lending rate by 1.08% to 5.58% in late November. However, there is skepticism about how much benefit the rate reduction will bring. More crucial than the rate reduction is the question of how much the banks will lend and to what concerns.

Chinese officialdom has become fearful of social and political instability, as well they should be. The Chinese political system doesn't deal well with popular challenges. In recent years, 70 to 80 thousand political demonstrations and riots have been reported annually, largely sparked by economic grievances. For example, 9,000 taxi drivers in Chongqing went on strike in November damaging cars and impeding the flow of traffic until party officials agreed to address their concerns. Since that time, teachers, factory workers, and other members of China's new middle class have stopped working until their demands are satisfied.

Chinese believe that the number "8" represents good

luck. After all, it was not by chance that the Beijing Olympics started on the eighth day of the eighth month in two thousand and eight at eight o'clock in the evening. If there is anything to the notion, the better that party leaders "protect eight," the less political turmoil China will bear.

Serve the People
Honolulu, June 8, 2008

The Sichuan Earthquake, measured at 7.9 on the Richter scale on May 12, 2008, has helped to put the 73 million strong Chinese Communist Party (CCP) back in touch with the 1.3 billion Chinese it allegedly serves.

Immortalized in a 1944 speech by Mao Tse-tung, the notion "serve the people" (weirenminfuwu) became a fundamental principle of the CCP. The party closely aligned itself with the masses by promoting and adhering to the Maoist dictum.

Although the party has certainly provided China with colossal economic growth, if only to maintain its own supremacy in Chinese society, many Chinese and international observers feel that the party has lost its ability to identify with the typical man or woman on the street. Without countervailing forces such as a free press, independent judiciary, open elections, and a legislature that is still largely considered a rubber stamp, corruption runs rampant throughout the party and clearly takes precedence over serving the people.

China's spectacular growth has provided party officials with no shortage of opportunities to abuse their positions for financial gain by participating in real estate schemes using public funds, by breaking land lease contracts with farmers for the benefit of developers who wish to build a factory or shopping mall, and by looking the other way in cases involving contemptuous labor practices. General Secretary of the CCP Hu Jintao's prescription to stymie corruption through use of the party's central disciplinary committee and promotion of the *Eight Honors and Eight Disgraces* as a moral code for party cadre has achieved little.

His biggest "bust" was the arrest of Shanghai First Secretary Chen Liangyu, who with other Shanghai officials had used pension funds to invest in real estate deals. As guilty as Chen was, the real motivation for his removal was purely political. Chen was aligned with the Shanghai clique of the CCP that opposed many of Hu's policies. Hu's approach to corruption is not unique in that "corruption fighting" is an often used pretext to silence political opponents. Meanwhile, political friends keep busily involved in whatever scams they might be involved in.

Heading a government that is not known for quick action and bound by bureaucratic red tape, a mere ninety minutes after the quake, Premier Wen Jiabao was on a plane bound for the stricken area. Wen is known as the "people's premier" in that he is considered modest, engaging, and does not convey the elitist image that other national leaders often do. Moreover, he specialized in geomechanics at the Beijing Institute of Geology as a college student.

Arriving in Sichuan, Wen personally directed rescue operations, at one time in tears, for five days. On the day after his arrival, with a megaphone in hand, he was shouting encouragement to those trapped in rubble and motivating rescuers by proclaiming, "So long as there is a glimmer of hope we shall not rest."

Wen ordered 135,000 troops to the area to help in rescue efforts. The troops lacked proper training in rescue operations and adequate amounts of appropriate equipment, yet they were highly motivated and earnest in their attempt to save as many quake victims as possible. Thankfully, they were. To date, the statistics are 69,107 confirmed dead; 373,577 injured; 18,230 missing; and 4.8 million homeless. Some estimates of economic loss run as high as 86 billion dollars.

Realizing the magnitude of the tragedy, the CCP soon jettisoned its normal caution. National and international journalists were given unfettered access to the quake zone and allowed to report whatever they wished—quite a decision due to the nuclear weapons research facilities in Mianyang.

Non-government organizations (NGOs) are in their infancy in China where the government remains politically wary of large ones. Nevertheless, any controls that might have been considered were dropped, and the party controlled press acknowledged the role of NGOs and their volunteers.

More startling was that despite the political difficulties in the relationship between China and Taiwan, rescue volunteers from Taiwan NGOs were gladly welcomed and among the first from outside China to arrive. Taiwan-based China Airlines flew 100 tons of supplies from Taiwan to Sichuan for Taiwan's Tzu Chi Foundation and the Republic of China Red Cross. Politics aside, Taiwan has amassed enormous experience in dealing with earthquake disasters.

Notwithstanding China's constantly reminding Japan about the savagery of its military invasion of China during World War II, Chinese and Japanese alike were completely bamboozled when China requested Japanese military help to move survivors and supplies. Japan simply didn't know how to deal with the request. One moment they were going to comply, the next not. Finally, Japan said that it wouldn't send military aircraft due to concern about its lingering war image raised in Chinese websites. However, they would send chartered aircraft.

China's epic economic growth has helped to foster a new sense of national pride shared by most Chinese. That pride was carried to a higher level when China was awarded the 2008 Summer Olympics, which to the Chinese represents the recognition of its new global status. If there was any doubt, the emotional Chinese response to demonstrations against the torch relay in London and Paris, and calls for world leaders to boycott the opening ceremony of the Olympics, further underlined China's burgeoning national pride and demand for international respect. A special session of public mourning dedicated to the quake victims was held in cavernous Tiananmen Square. It was the largest expression of mourning since Mao's death. At the end of the session, the crowds spontaneously launched into chanting patriotic slogans, concluding with a resounding "Long Live China."

A new sense of trust in the party combined with a growing nationalism might well make China a more challenging country for all to deal with, if indeed the current level of both remains.

Equal Players, Responsible Stakeholders, or Global Competitors?
Honolulu, May 14, 2006

As important as they may seem, high profile meetings of world leaders are often well scripted, carefully planned photo opportunities designed to send a message to domestic audiences, often yielding few concrete results.

President Hu Jintao's first visit (April 18-21, 2006) to the U.S. as Chinese president was well thought out in advance. Long before he left Beijing, Hu dispatched Politburo member and well known international negotiator, Vice-Premier Wu Yi to the U.S. with a delegation of over two hundred leading Chinese business executives. Wu's delegation first stopped in Hawaii to pen a memorandum of understanding with Governor Linda Lingle to promote Chinese tourism to the islands.

Chinese tourists visiting Hawaii would not only create another market for Hawaii tourism but also offer some help in reducing America's $201 billion trade deficit with the People's Republic. However, increased Chinese tourism depends on the U.S. government liberalizing its visa regulations for mainland Chinese tourists, which is somewhat unlikely given the long-term effort to liberalize tourist visas for South Korean tourists.

From Hawaii, Wu proceeded to Washington, D.C. to meet with Secretary of Commerce Carlos Gutierrez and United States Trade Representative Rob Porter to discuss ways of reducing China's trade surplus. High on the agenda was the protection of U.S. intellectual property rights (computer software, recorded music products, and movies) for which the Chinese presented a 48-page document, *China's Action Plan on Intellectual Property Rights Protection 2006*. Moreover, Chinese government contracts would be opened for U.S. bidding, and the ban on U.S. beef exports would be lifted. While in Washington, other members of Wu's delegation visited 14 cities signing contracts totaling $16.1 billion in purchases of software, farm goods, and Boeing aircraft. In international terms, the $16.1 billion is an insignificant amount. One quarter of that amount is represented by purchase of the aircraft, many parts of which are produced by Boeing's Chinese partners.

Arriving in Everett, Washington, President Hu was out to win Americans over. Alighting from his aircraft, he greeted the crowd with a wave while holding the hand of his wife, Liu Yongqing. Other than young lovers strolling on Shanghai's moonlit Bund, such a public display of affection is unthinkable in China, especially for a sixty-seven year old of Hu's stature. The nerdy-looking Hu was introduced by Microsoft cofounder and Chairman Bill Gates who touted the President's engineering background and government service, omitting his tenure as First Secretary of the Chinese Communist Party (CCP) of Tibet where he won kudos from the late patriarch Deng Xiaoping for quickly suppressing a political demonstration in 1988. Afterwards, Deng catapulted Hu onto the Politburo standing committee, the CCP's highest decision making body, where most members were in their 70s or 80s; Hu was only forty-nine. During his West Coast stay, Hu was always addressed or referred to as "President;" however, the source of his real power is his position as General Secretary of the CCP and Chairman of the Central Military Affairs Commission, titles which might create a negative impression among the American public.

A common Chinese strategy in seeking better relations with a society or country that have second thoughts about a closer relationship with China is to curry favor with prominent business leaders. Such was their strategy in the return of Hong Kong. Currently, the Chinese seek to prevent Taiwan from further advocating independence by reemphasizing the economic benefits Taiwanese businesses derive from Mainland investments. Japan's economic recovery has largely been fuelled by trade with China. As a result, key Japanese business leaders are putting pressure on the Japanese government to improve its poor relationship with China.

In that American big business has been a consistent key driver of American China policy, it's not surprising that Hu's reception at Boeing by business leaders was so effusive. In the reception line was former Secretary of State Henry A. Kissinger, architect of America's opening to China in 1972. The former secretary now runs Kissinger and Associates, an international consulting firm catering to large corporate clients doing business abroad, and often is referred to as America's leading "panda hugger" for his unswerving advocacy of the Sino-American relationship. No wonder then that in television coverage, Hu was shown giving the panda hugger, a big hug—another un-Chinese gesture.

Hu's warm reception by big business leaders in Washington State stood in stark contrast with the cool government reception he received in Washington, D.C. Hu's originally planned trip to the U.S. was postponed because of Hurricane Katrina, prompting a number of administration insiders to quip, "Thank God for Katrina." The U.S. seems conflicted by China. Yes, it wants a vibrant business relationship but feels that China often does not play by the rules and spirit of international trade. Based on the *2006 Quadrennial Defense Review,* the U.S. sees China as a key security threat and is far from accepting Beijing's view that its growing global influence is a "peaceful rise." Yet, the U.S. has begun to call China a "responsible stakeholder" in global politics and is seeking ways to mutually control nuclear proliferation and terrorism while denying China the sense of equality it seeks.

Both Presidents Hu and Bush face uncertain domestic challenges and had hoped to use the summit to bolster their respective domestic standings. Despite its economic liberalization and reintegration into the world starting in the late 70s, China is a politically fragile country where the CCP's monopoly on power is confronted by a growing record number of riots and demonstrations sparked by land rights issues, party corruption, and inequitable distribution of wealth between those living in developed coastal cities and the countryside.

To maintain popular legitimacy, the CCP not only needs to keep China on a path of continual economic development, but it also must show that under its leadership, China is a highly respected member of the global community equal in stature to any other nation. President Bush's job approval rating is at an all time low of 36%. Awash in popular discontent over Iraq, high gas prices, and the likelihood that the Democratic Party will take control of the U.S. House of Representatives in the November 2006 mid-term elections, Bush's second term is not going well at all.

In the end, neither president got much of what they wanted. When planning to visit the President of the U.S., world leaders angle for an invitation to Bush's Crawford, Texas, ranch to convey to their home audiences that they have a special relationship with the President. Hu declined an invitation to the ranch. Despite rhetoric to the contrary, Chinese tend to look down at anything related to the countryside. The countryside is generally considered culturally backward and lacking sophistication. To the Chinese, a state visit to Washington, D.C., centered on the White House, complete with all the trappings and formality that proper protocol requires, would have a much more positive symbolic impact on Chinese television viewers than a trip to dusty Crawford. Moreover, Hu would show that China was an equal to the U.S.

Instead of a White House State Dinner, Hu got a one hour White House luncheon, reviewed the Old Guard Fife and Drum Corps perform on the White House south lawn, and received a twenty-one gun salute. While that might have served as some form of consolation, it was marred by the White House announcing the playing of the Chinese national anthem as the national anthem of the "Republic of China," the official name given to the government on Taiwan, rather than as the national anthem of the "People's Republic of China." Things got even worse as an erstwhile member of the press corps displayed a Falungong (a religious group outlawed in China) banner and loudly heckled Hu as he was making his comments on the south lawn. The heckler, Dr. Wang Wenyi, a pathologist originally from Northeastern China and now a New York City resident, has a record of heckling Chinese leaders. Although Bush apologized, given her history and the resulting embarrassment to Hu, the Chinese felt that the U.S. did not take sufficient care in making preparations for Hu's visit. If nothing else, in their joint press conference, Hu did get a clear statement, "I do not support Taiwan independence," from Bush that must have made him happy.

Although distracted by Iraq and having low expectations, the U.S. still wanted a lot from Hu's visit. High on the U.S.'s list was revaluation of China's currency, the yuan. The U.S. maintains that China unfairly manipulates the exchange rate of its currency in order to sell its products abroad at a cheaper price. Reflecting this is America's huge trade deficit with China and the adverse impact on certain sectors of the U.S. economy such as the furniture and garment industries. Hu showed no interest in revaluation. In fairness, he could not since any revaluation would result in a loss of Chinese jobs. He did suggest, however, that in the future China's economic development would be more based on expanded domestic demand than on exports.

A key component of U.S. foreign policy is the advancement of democracy. Hu contended, without suggesting how, that China was indeed democratic and talked about the future need for "managed democracy" and "supervised democracy" without spelling out the nature of either. He reiterated China's commitment to democracy in a speech at Yale University. At a time when Americans are concerned about abuses at Guantanamo and Abu Gharib plus the Patriot Act and domestic spying, the U.S. risks the appearance of creating a double standard by too strongly advocating democracy. Then again, one wonders just how vigorously democracy can be promoted to a key creditor who has shown no real interest in such a system.

The Chinese showed little interest in exerting more

influence on North Korea to denuclearize or trying to persuade the Sudanese government to halt genocide in Darfur. Sudan is a Chinese energy supplier. The U.S. and China have clearly divergent positions on Iran. The U.S. does not accept the Iranian government's position that their nuclear development is for peaceful purposes. The U.S. and the European Union want to see Iranian nuclear development suspended, and have threatened to seek sanctions in the UN Security Council where China maintains veto power. China sees Iran as an oil supplier and has invested heavily in the country's oil infrastructure.

It might not seem that Chinese diplomacy is on a roll, looking at Hu's trip to the U.S. However, after he left the U.S., he went to Saudi Arabia, a key Chinese energy supplier and another major U.S. creditor who shares a similar lack of interest in democracy, where he was warmly greeted and signed energy, trade, and security agreements. Iran emphasized its wish to become a full member in the Chinese driven Shanghai Cooperation Organization, which is a growing multilateral defense organization seeking to limit U.S. influence in Central Asia. And it was announced that China would accelerate oil exploration with Cuba in an area only fifty miles from the Florida Keys. Meanwhile, back in Washington, D.C., the Bush administration remains locked on to Iraq while fumbling for a way to more successfully deal with China's rise.

William E. Sharp, Jr.

Qiao Chu's China
Beijing, China, January 14, 2007

As a manifestation of China's decade plus phenomenal growth rate of 9.5% per annum, China's middle class is experiencing similar growth. Born into this new lap of luxury and comfort, sixteen year old Qiao Chu is living a life of comfort complete with all of the creature comforts that her mother and father could only have dreamed of growing up.

Qiao Chu was born in Changchun, the capital of Northeast China's Jilin Province. During the 1930s and 1940s, Japan ruled the area through its invention of the "Manchukuo" (Manchuria) puppet state. Therefore, at the time that the People's Republic of China was established on October 1, 1949, the Northeast was one of China's few relatively developed economic centers benefiting from the factories and steel mills that the Japanese had built. Changchun itself became known as a center of the Chinese automobile industry with the Red Flag Automobile Company that made limousines for high level cadre and a center for China's motion picture industry, hosting the Changchun Movie Studio. But while the rest of China has boomed, the Northeast has not. China's engines of economic development and focus of foreign direct investment are in the Pearl River Delta (between Hong Kong and Guangzhou) and the greater Shanghai area. Today's Northeast has become known as China's rustbelt.

Despite the dwindling fortunes of the Northeast, Qiao

Chu's mother and father remained committed to the area and were both employed in one of China's leading banks, making comfortable but not large salaries. Her father's parents took care of Qiao Chu while her parents were at work. When she was ready to start school, her grandparents and a generous aunt living in America made it financially possible for Qiao Chu to attend a prestigious private school, where she soon excelled in English.

Qiao Chu's mother's sister and husband had moved to Shenzhen (across the border dividing China proper and Hong Kong) where salaries were typically twice as large as those paid in the Northeast. Soon Qiao Chu's parents began to look beyond the Northeast for better wage earning opportunities. They thought of joining their relatives in Shenzhen, but they soon realized that Beijing offered good job opportunities with salaries just as good as those paid in Shenzhen and was closer to their parents who chose to remain in Changchun.

Moving to Beijing used to be nearly impossible. With continued economic development has come the liberalization of the *hukou* system, which was a strictly enforced administrative system controlling in which cities and towns people could live. Appreciating that the hukou system might again become strict, Qiao Chu's parents headed off to Beijing to find new jobs. Her mother found a job in a brand new high rise office building, as an administrative supervisor in a telecommunications company, and her father works as a public relations executive in a high tech company. In U.S. dollars, Qiao Chu's mother makes $500 a month, over twice as much as she made in Changchun; her father makes close to $1,250 a month, nearly six times more than he made before arriving in Beijing. He also receives a year end bonus, calculated on the basis of how well the company performed during the year.

A year or so after getting settled in their new jobs in Beijing, Qiao Chu's hardworking and thrifty parents, with a loan from a relative, paid the Chinese equivalent of $80,000 U.S. dollars cash for a condominium, one hour from the Gate of Heavenly Peace (Tian An Men) in central Beijing. Privately owned residential real estate is quite different from the square shaped, state owned, architecturally monotonous, dark, high rise buildings in which work units used to assign employees apartments. Qiao Chu's father proudly tells everyone that they live in a French style dwelling.

Approaching their complex, one certainly has the sensation that they have just been whisked to Paris. The wrought iron entrance gate looks like a gate at the Elysee Palace. Beyond the gate is a miniature Arc d'Triumphe, amid a wide open, grassy area for leisurely strolling that is reminiscent of Paris's Jardin des Tuileries. The complex is organized into modules, each three or four stories high, made of a material that looks like red brick and in which there are different size apartments. At least 75% of the residents own cars, and many families have two cars.

Qiao Chu's parents' unit is approximately 1,200 sq. ft. It has three bedrooms, two bathrooms, a dining room with chandelier, wooden floors throughout, air conditioning, and a kitchen loaded with a wide variety of electrical appliances including a dishwasher, a washer, and a dryer. Although the unit is on the fourth floor, there is no elevator and no trash chute. One stays in shape by negotiating the steps and walking the trash out to the bin. Back in the unit, there are two televisions, a CD player, a portable DVD player, and a huge aquarium. It is all quite a world apart from the state housing where her parents grew up, and often had to share cooking, bathing, and toilet facilities with neighbors.

As comfortable as the digs might seem, Qiao Chu doesn't see much of them. After moving to Beijing, she enrolled in another private school that is about two hours away. There she shares a dormitory room with five other coeds. She is only home every other weekend, during summer vacations, and Chinese New Year. The school is more competitive than her old school in Changchun, and she has to work hard for her grades; however, English still seems to come to her quickly. About the school uniforms: "They're not so beautiful," she says. When she isn't studying or attending class, she likes to experiment with make-up, and, like any U.S. teenager, talk on her cellular phone or exchange text messages. Does she have a boy friend? "No, my mother would kill me," she says. Asked if China is a superpower, she instantly replies, "No." Soliciting her opinion about America, she just as quickly responds, "It always fights."

As for her future, other than traveling to the U.S., she is not sure what she wants to do. Her father would like her to attend China's most prestigious university, Beijing

University, and her mother would like her to become a diplomat. Her aunt in the U.S. feels Qiao Chu could become an excellent chef.

Whatever future road she travels, it will be one that she selects and not one that the government unilaterally dictates, as was typical in China when her mother and father were growing up. Nor will she likely have to endure "being sent down" as was typical for her parents' generation. Being sent down was a practice during China's Cultural Revolution where urban youth and adults were both sent to the countryside to do menial agricultural jobs to purify their revolutionary spirit and to cleanse them of their urban, bourgeois ways. Rather than promoting itself as a revolutionary society, Qiao Chu's China is a burgeoning superpower that blends market economics with socialist rhetoric.

To both Qiao Chu and China, the benefits are greater.

Chinese Patriot: From Red Guard to Global Entrepreneur
Beijing, China, August 12, 2007

Employing over thirty employees, housed in a spacious spic and span office in trendy, upscale Northeastern Beijing, it is hard to believe that Liu Ping, fifty-five, founder and general manager of Star Professional Programs was once a "Red Guard" who passionately idolized Mao Tse-tung.

Born in 1955 in Northeast China's Liaoning Province, she is the eldest of four children, including a sister and two brothers. Her mother and father were people of very modest means. Mining might be a well paid job in the U.S. It has never been in China. Answering Mao's call to develop China, her father and mother, both loyal members of the Chinese Communist Party since before the establishment of the People's Republic in 1949, moved from the Northeast to backward Guizhou Province, in the Southwest, to work in mines.

Ping has a unique view of Chinese political events, having lived through everyone since the Great Leap Forward (GLF), from 1958 to 1961, when Mao encouraged peasants to smelt steel in their backyards in order to rapidly surpass Britain in steel production. The GLF was not only a colossal failure at producing steel, it also led to the mass starvation of an estimated thirty million Chinese. Ping relates how Party cadre blamed the failure of the GLF on weather conditions. Nevertheless, her father felt great pride in seeing that steel produced from the natural resources in the mine he was working was used in construction projects in Southwest China.

Ping was attending junior high school in Guizhou when the most profound political event of post-1949 China was sweeping through the country. The Great Proletarian Cultural Revolution (1966-1976) was a nationwide attempt by Mao to purge the party of capitalist roaders—those more interested in building China's economy than with creating the new socialist man or philosophizing about Marxist-Stalinist-Maoist

Thought.

To ensure that revolution was passed on to China's youth, Mao created the Red Guards (hongweibing) who were to study, learn, and promote revolution to help ensure that party members taking the capitalist road were permanently extirpated.

Because of her singing and dancing talent, Ping was recruited by a Red Guard propaganda team while only twelve years old. As a member of a propaganda team, she acted in skits, sang songs, and performed dances all designed to inculcate audiences in revolutionary Maoist Thought. Asked why she joined the Red Guards, she responded, "There was not really any choice. They came to get me one day, and my parents didn't say a thing. They couldn't, given the nature of the times. Everyone had unswerving faith in Mao. It was a national craze." Listening to her relate her Red Guard experiences, it is easy to tell that from a very early age she has had a deep love for China, which membership in the Red Guards allowed her to express.

Mao himself ultimately acknowledged that the Cultural Revolution had gotten out of control and called in the People's Liberation Army to restore order. Ping began to lose interest after seeing her father paraded through the streets as a capitalist roader.

Her Red Guard days having ended, Ping went to work in a factory making explosives and soon became the only female underground mining electrician. Having won the praise of her fellow workers as a model worker, despite having a relative who had been a supporter of the Chinese

Nationalists, they recommended her for admission to Guizhou University where she wanted to study electrical engineering. However, the demands of the state prevailed, and she was directed to study English in which she had no interest or background.

After graduating in 1976, Ping was a junior high school English teacher in Guizhou Province for a few years. Had she lost her revolutionary zeal? It seems not in that she taught students many of Mao's quotes in English.

In 1978-1979, with Deng Xiaoping restored to power, China opened itself to the world. Tourists from abroad began to flow into China. Using her English skills, Ping became a government official, working for a large state tourist corporation that welcomed tourists from abroad. Working for the government gave her a good foundation in the tourist industry. Unfortunately for China, the notion of everyone eats from the same pot encouraged lackadaisical work habits, which saw many employees reading newspapers, drinking tea, smoking cigarettes, and generally avoiding work most of the day. Ping, on the other hand, was an ambitious employee with an outstanding record of nailing down important accounts.

In 2001, China joined the World Trade Organization (WTO). To Ping, the WTO represented an opportunity for her to run a travel agency based on internationally accepted standards of good management. She took a calculated risk by resigning from the government and set out to start her own company. If successful, her company would give her more money, allow her to develop her management skills, provide for family members, provide for herself in her old age, and pass something on to her son.

Like a lot of Chinese entrepreneurs just starting out, Ping borrowed 1.5 million Chinese yuan (about $20,000 U.S. dollars) from her friends and soon rented a small office. Securing a license was a tricky process. She effectively rented a license from a travel company that had gone out of business in order to operate her company. Finally, after two and one-half years, the license was all hers, and her business has been a success ever since.

Her company, Star Professional Programs, specializes in highly tailored tours for single travelers or groups of international travelers with particular interests, for example, groups of lawyers, doctors, educators, and business executives from various industries. She also organizes conferences. Central to her management style is long-term planning, constant staff training, and a deep concern for branding. If that sounds like something straight out of an MBA, it might very well be in that Ping just completed an MBA program.

Her success is obvious and she can often be found working at her desk long after staff members have gone home. When she goes to work in the morning and finally returns home to Beijing's posh Shunyi Villas, where she owns three units, she is chauffeured in her gleaming, brand spanking new Mercedes S-Class. Interestingly, she calls herself "highly successful," but also "middle class." She readily admits, as do other Chinese, that one of China's biggest problems is unequal distribution of income.

It is easy to assume that she is a member of the CCP given her parents' membership, her Red Guard experience, and that she exemplifies the success of many Chinese economic policies. She is not. She has been repeatedly coaxed by many party officials, but she has consistently declined, wishing to avoid internal party politics and the demands on time that membership would require.

However, she has not removed herself from politics. The CCP is the only party legally enabled to hold power; however, there are eight non-Communist democratic parties that have been in existence before 1949 and helped the CCP come to power. Ping is an active member of the Jiusan Society (JS), which maintains a membership of 88,000 and is chaired by Han Qide. Like the other democratic parties, JS discusses a wide variety of problems confronting contemporary China. Once they have arrived at a consensus, they bring their concerns to the attention of the local committee of the Chinese People's Political Consultative Conference, referred to by some as the upper house of the Chinese legislature, who consider the merits of the issue and either try to solve the problem or dismiss it.

Ping feels that liberal Western democracy will not come to China any time during her life and stresses that given the geographic size, huge population, and uneven economic and human development of China that such democracy is not appropriate. Many Chinese see Western democracy as being dysfunctional and give greater importance to maintaining unity and stability. She does, however, stress that decision making in China is not simply one person deciding everything such as was typical in Mao's day. Consensual decision making involves far greater numbers of citizens.

Ping is performing a far greater service to China than merely joining the party. Internationally, she is the Chair of the Beijing Chapter of People to People International, which was started by President Dwight D. Eisenhower to enhance intercultural communication. Through the organization and her company, she has an opportunity to explain China to hundreds of influential international tourists each year. In her words, "I want others to understand China." Thus, the girl who joined the Red Guard out of a love for China is the successful woman entrepreneur who still loves her country today.

An Indecent Proposal
Honolulu, August 14, 2005

If the China National Offshore Oil Corporation had not withdrawn its offer for United Oil of California (UNOCAL), Washington should have blocked the deal.

China's long-term strategic goal is to be the dominant power in Asia. To do so, it must reduce the influence of America in Asia, secure ocean passageways for the transport of oil, and guarantee its access to natural resources. These goals often overlap.

Chinese diplomacy has been very busy and successful

in recent months settling old disputes. Witness the newfound friendship between Indonesia and China, Chinese maneuvering to close U.S. bases in Central Asia, and the resolution of long standing border issues with India. In all cases, the countries involved had improving relations with America, possessed oil and/or other natural resources, or were geographically situated to disrupt oil transportation from the Middle East or Southeast Asia to Chinese ports.

The Japanese-American relationship is very close and becoming closer in its security aspects. Chinese government condoned anti-Japanese demonstrations in 2005 were ostensibly in protest of Japan's failure to again apologize for its criminal behavior during World War II, but in reality, the Chinese were protesting Japan's bid for a permanent seat on the Security Council of the United Nations, a bid which was backed by the U.S. Given the U.S. support of Japan's bid and the fact that Japan so closely follows the U.S. lead in its post-World War II foreign policy, and is the foundation of U.S. defense posture in Asia, the protest was indirectly anti-American. Muddying the image of Japan will ultimately help to reduce both Japanese and American influence in Asia.

With oil, natural gas, and fish resources estimated at one trillion dollars, China claims virtually all of the South China Sea as its own, despite protest from countries in the area. In 1974, China militarily seized the oil and natural gas rich Paracel Islands from the then Republic of South Vietnam. A study conducted by the Chinese Ministry of Geology and Mineral Resources estimated that Spratly Island oil deposits and natural gas reserves at 17.7 billion tons. In comparison, Kuwait's deposits stand at 13 billion tons. China claims ownership of the one hundred plus islands in the group as does Taiwan and Vietnam. Brunei, Malaysia, and the Philippines each claim at least a few of the islands. Periodic military clashes have taken place between China and other claimants. In 1995, despite Filipino diplomatic protest, China militarily took control of Mischief Reef (in the Spratly Islands), which is within the 200-mile Filipino exclusive economic zone and then fortified it.

Both island groups occupy strategic positions astride the main sea lanes leading north, from the eastern end of the Malacca Straits to Chinese ports. One half of all supertanker tonnage passes through the Spratly Islands each year. If China wishes, then it can use its naval forces to block the transport of Middle Eastern or Southeast Asian oil to Japanese and Korean ports. The Chinese government is also reported to have leased a naval base on an approach to the Malacca Straits from Myanmar (Burma).

UNOCAL represents U.S. influence in Asia through its investments in Thailand, Myanmar, Indonesia, Vietnam and the Philippines. Generally, it has been a good corporate citizen and large employer. The totality of its investments has a profound political, economic, and military effect on the Southeast Asian countries and people where it does business. Would China play the same role? The Chinese were only interested in UNOCAL's Asian operations, even offering to sell its

American based assets if the deal went through. Many of UNOCAL's Asian oil and natural gas contracts are in locations of similar waterborne strategic value. For example, the Yadana gas fields off of the Myanmar coast in the Andaman Sea and control of six thousand square miles of water off of the South Coast of Vietnam. Supplanting UNOCAL as a leading partner in the building of the 748 mile natural gas pipeline from Turkmenistan through Afghanistan to Pakistan would give China great advantages and influence in an area of growing importance to the U.S.

Given China's trove of dollar denominated foreign reserves, there will be future offers to buy U.S. corporations and assets throughout the world. Each offer must be closely reviewed for its security and economic implications, not simply a fast buck.

Only a Foolish China would Attack Taiwan
Honolulu, June 10, 2007

It is widely assumed China would militarily attack Taiwan if the island declared independence, held a public referendum to institute a new constitution, or changed or did away with too many of the symbols that historically associate it with China, such as the Republic of China (ROC) flag. However, such an attack could be to China's disadvantage.

According to Robert S. Ross, writing in the March/

April 2006 edition of *Foreign Policy*, the Taiwanese Independence Movement has lost much of its allure. Those who supported strong independence advocate, President Chen Shui-bian in his first presidential victory have since abandoned him. The public is more interested in Taiwan's economic life and sees no significant material gain in independence.

President Chen has exhausted his political capital in Washington, and it is unlikely that any other major country or many of the twenty-four minor states that recognize Taiwan as the Republic of China would automatically transfer their recognition to a "Republic of Taiwan." In fact, not all of those minor states that are so dependent on ROC largesse voted in favor of Taiwan's tenth attempt to join the World Health Organization in early May. Admission of a Republic of Taiwan into the UN is a clear non-starter.

Because of the publicity given modernization and the recent 18% budget increase, the People's Liberation Army (PLA) is thought to be invincible. While it could use its eight to nine hundred Dong Feng (East Wind) missiles to wreak great economic destruction to Taiwan, it lacks the amphibious training and capacity to transport enough occupying troops to Taiwan.

Maintaining a force of 290,000 active duty members and 1.6 million reserves, the ROC military is working hard to upgrade its military preparedness. A key to the defense of Taiwan is the 146 F-16s, 57 French Mirages, and 128 Taiwan developed Indigenous Defense Fighters. Fighter pilot training is being extended from six to eight months. In mid-May, Taiwan concluded its annual Han Kuang (Han Glory) live fire military training exercises. A PRC attack on Taiwan would be met by a ROC cruise and ballistic missile counter attack designed to destroy Shanghai and coastal areas that have experienced such phenomenal economic growth. Both the U.S. and Japan maintain strong relations with Taiwan. U.S. naval assets in Japan and troops in Okinawa would be involved in Taiwan's defense, creating a situation that China could not win.

A military failure to bring Taiwan under the control of the PRC would likely force the leadership to resign and weaken the Chinese Communist Party's legitimacy, which many Chinese already question due to ever growing corruption.

Even if China were able to subdue Taiwan, ruling the island would be a difficult if not impossible task for the PRC. Those that grew up in Taiwan have been taught to despise the Chinese Communists from the time they entered elementary school. Moreover, most people in Taiwan consider themselves "Taiwanese," not Chinese. They are fully cognizant that Taiwan enjoys a burgeoning democracy, a free flow of information, and is more economically developed than Mainland China with a more enviable life style.

The Mainland Chinese Nationalists were warmly welcomed to Taiwan at the conclusion of World War II. However, Taiwanese hopes were soon dashed by Nationalist corruption and repression, which resulted in the 228 Incident of 1947. The bloody Nationalist military repression of the incident resulted in an estimated ten to twenty thousand Taiwanese deaths, and helped to build an inseparable wall between "waishengren" (those from the mainland) and "benshengren" (those born in Taiwan). PRC control of Taiwan affected through military means would likely have a similar effect.

Since the founding of the PRC in 1949, China has sought to consolidate its rule in the Xinjiang Autonomous Region. There is still no light at the end of the tunnel, despite the government's placing economic power in the hands of the people as a strategy to suborn them. Control of Tibet has been equally as elusive since the mid-50s.

An arms race would be set into motion throughout Northeast Asia. Japan would be further impelled to become a military power, seriously consider an active role in the U.S.-sponsored Theater Missile Defense Program, and contemplate the development of nuclear weapons. At a minimum, Japan would be driven further into the arms of the U.S., dashing any Chinese hope of separating the two to enhance China's regional clout. South Korea would give deep second thought to its burgeoning relationship with China. Any Chinese idea of morphing the Six-Party Talks into a Northeast Asian regional security apparatus that might ultimately lead to the withdrawal of U.S. troops from South Korea, and possibly Japan, would be a great set back.

In Southeast Asia, China's hard work to improve its image and to earn credibility with Association of Southeast Asian Nations member states—many of whom still don't trust China's long-term intentions—would be for naught. Particularly important would be Indonesia, which as the most populous country in the region is generally seen as the most important country in Southeast Asia and the one with the most nightmarish memories of China, due to the close relationship between China and former President Sukarno.

In South Asia, India would be strongly influenced to create a closer security relationship with the U.S.

All of this is not to say that Taiwan has nothing to worry about. Clearly, it has fallen behind in its military preparedness due to internecine political squabbling between the Pan-Blue coalition dominated legislature and the Pan-Green coalition led by President Chen Shui-bian. Nor should Taiwanese independence advocates automatically assume that the U.S. would come to their defense as they persistently taunt China. China has often bitterly complained that U.S. policy seeks to geographically contain it. A PRC attack on Taiwan would only realize China's worst fear: unfriendly countries on its borders in league with the U.S.

The Yuan Rises
Honolulu, August 19, 2005

Appreciation of the Chinese yuan against the dollar will do little to improve the trade deficit with China. The 2.190% managed float is based on a secret basket of currencies and allows for the Chinese government to intervene if the daily exchange rate should increase by more than 0.3%.

The Plaza Accord signed at the Plaza Hotel in New York City on September 22, 1985, brought about the appreciation of the Japanese yen against the dollar in an unsuccessful attempt to balance America's huge trade deficit with Japan. The cause of the trade deficit with both Japan and China is voracious American consumerism. Owing to a low savings rate, Americans have a high amount of disposable income. Despite a 51% appreciation of the yen against the dollar, American consumers continued to buy Japanese goods. No matter how much the yuan appreciates against the dollar, American manufacturers will not be able to compete against cheap Chinese goods.

The irony of the yuan's appreciation is that it might actually increase the trade deficit while hurting U.S. attempts to keep inflation down. Off the peg, China will still maintain a trade surplus; however, it will be less motivated to finance U.S. debt and provide financial backing for low cost mortgages by purchasing U.S. treasury bonds. Heretofore, China was willing to accept a low yield on its treasury bonds to help ward off criticism about its trade surplus. The U.S. will have to pay higher interest rates to maintain Chinese interest and to attract other investors.

In reality, the revaluation is a shallow, short term political victory giving bragging rights to the Bush Administration, and Treasury Secretary Snow in particular, that they took "concrete steps to set the trade deficit right." When it becomes obvious that the revaluation has not solved the problem, tensions between the U.S. and China will again play center stage. It is easier to point a finger at another country, rather than at a voter.

Trade deficits can be the kindling for international dispute. We need a new system of calculating trade deficits that is based on a globally negotiated method of calculation, universally applied and that more accurately reflects which companies and nations ultimately retain profits. Many exports coming from China to the U.S. are actually products manufactured in U.S.-owned and capitalized factories in China.

Trading Shame for Respect
Honolulu, September 14, 2008

The Beijing Olympics left Chinese and international audiences alike in gaping awe. To the Chinese, the seventeen-day athletic competition was the fulfillment of a hundred-year dream to overcome the humiliation dealt it by avaricious foreign powers from the time of China's defeat in the Opium War.

Zhang Yimou, China's best known movie director, precisely choreographed the opening ceremony, accented by dazzling pyrotechnics and colorful costumes highlighting China's cultural and historic achievements. It was a hands down artistic masterpiece.

However spectacular the opening ceremony might have been, China's real purpose for hosting the 29th Olympiad was to let the world know that in the short span of thirty years, it had broken out of its international isolation. China had become a burgeoning world power flush with a trillion dollars in foreign reserves, plus growing global political clout, military might, and seductive soft power.

The Olympics was clearly political. Whatever country hosts the quadrennial event, it has never been purely about athletic competition. The Beijing Olympics was even more political given the great importance China attached to it. The nation shelled out $42 billion to host it in high fashion.

For example, the Chinese government did not fulfill its promise to allow foreign journalists to go anywhere and to interview Chinese citizens without prior government approval. China announced its relaxed policy in January 2007. For the same year, the Foreign Correspondents Club of China reported 180 cases of government interference that resulted in members' arrest, confiscated memory cards and equipment, and even beatings. To top things off, President Hu Jintao had the temerity to invite a group of foreign journalists to a televised "talk story" session where he grandfatherly admonished them, "Don't politicize the spirit of the Olympics."

Hypocritically, China did exactly what it wanted the foreign journalists to not do. Staged in a Beijing theater, at the end of the Olympics, *Princess Wenchang* is a story about the marriage of a 7th Century Chinese princess to a Tibetan king. The political intent was unmistakably clear: All is well between China and Tibet. The message is impossible to accept, given the March riots in Tibet and the ongoing struggle between the Dalai Lama and the Chinese government.

The Olympics proved the ability of centralized state power to produce. The central government played the key role in securing the bid, creating the incomparable facilities, and the formation and execution of Operation 119 to recruit and train world class athletes in a wide variety of sports, many of which most Chinese have no interest in. All of this was accomplished while dealing with the disastrous aftermath of a number of large earthquakes in Southwest China, plus growing Tibetan and Uighur unrest.

On the other hand, it is equally clear that China was more interested in ends rather than in means when it came to creating the right image for the Beijing Olympics. Migrant laborers were summarily sent back to their villages to prevent any possible demonstration about their working conditions, and rural dwellers were prevented from travelling to Beijing to present petitions. To make way for Olympic facilities, neighborhoods were razed resulting in the involuntary displacement of nearly 15,000 residents, many of whom complained about inadequate compensation.

Many Chinese and foreigners wondered if the $42 billion spent on Olympics might have been better spent on building a new health care system in place of the health care system that fell apart in the countryside when China began to rationalize its economy. The supply of clean water remains a country wide problem. Economically, inland provinces such as Gansu and Qinghai remain far behind coastal provinces.

The International Olympic Committee felt awarding the Olympics to Beijing would help to usher in a period of greater concern for human rights and popular democracy. The attendance of President George W. Bush, Japanese Prime Minister Fukuda Yasuo, South Korean President Lee Myung-bak, and French President Nicolas Sarkozy underlined China's growing global commercial and political influence. China undoubtedly gained more of the international attention and the respect it sought. The leadership will likely try to parlay this into greater domestic support for its policies.

In at least the short term, however, the Olympics are unlikely to result in less control over the Tibetans, Uighurs, and religion. Democracy is not likely to benefit. Most Chinese realize that today's China is far more open and far less autocratic than in the past. One can freely pick their place of employment, own their own house, start their own business, plus travel and study abroad. It's a commonly held Western fallacy that China's growing middle class will clamor for democracy. In a forthcoming book that he co-edited on Asian views of democracy, noted China specialist Andrew Nathan argues that of the eight countries he researched, China was the most at ease with authoritarian rule. As I see it, China's key concern is to maintain stability. Moreover, they believe parliamentary democracy would result in the loss of their newly acquired material wealth. Thus, it is improbable that the Olympics will alter their views any time soon.

The lessons of the Beijing Olympics are clearly manifest for the U.S. and global community: Never underestimate China, as we have in our foreign policy with other Asian nations. Always remember that it has great determination to play a leading global role. It now has the financial resources, growing military capability, soft power, and commercial influence to achieve its political goals.

Whatever effect the Olympics might have on China will take time to discern. Nevertheless, as more and more Chinese jettison Marxism, the government seeks to strengthen Chinese nationalistic pride. The Olympics has clearly ramped up that pride; however, if the party and government don't rule in a manner that meets people's needs and expectations, that nationalism could well boom-a-rang and release a wave of uncontrollable fervor that would induce instability and prematurely end top level leaders' careers.

William E. Sharp, Jr.

Welcome to Qiao Chu's modern European-like home, one hour from central Beijing, China.

William E. Sharp, Jr.

Taiwan National Day 2006

Cheonggye Stream in Central Seoul, Korea

Random Views of Asia from the Mid-Pacific

William E. Sharp, Jr.

Chapter Three

TIBET

Little Hope for Change in Tibet
Honolulu, April 13, 2007

Recent media accounts have dwelt on the destruction and loss of life ensuing from the most recent uprising in the Tibet Autonomous Region and bordering Chinese provinces with predominately Tibetan populations. However, few have given much historical context.

Approximately 10% of China's population falls into one of fifty-five minority groups. Minority groups occupy 60% of China's total land area, albeit sparsely. For the most part, the minorities are situated in highly sensitive strategic areas. For example, along the Southern border with Vietnam, Laos, Myanmar (Burma), and Thailand; in the Southwest, Tibet shares a border with rival India; and in the Northwest Xinjiang, rich in oil, neighbors restive Islamic states in Central Asia and Russia, which once occupied this far flung corner of China.

Despite its growing reputation as a superpower, China is surprisingly fragile and could easily bifurcate into a group of competing regions. As much as Chinese leaders want to be recorded in history as the one who brought all areas that China lays claim to under the control of Beijing, they clearly recognize the potential for China to fragment. Hence, their concern in passing laws and in promoting propaganda themes that aver against "splittism," "separatism," and "independence." If they seem unduly "uptight," one only has to remember that it was Sun Yat-sen himself who warned that "the Chinese people have only family and clan solidarity; they do not have national spirit...they are just a heap of loose sand."

Once an empire stretching as far south as today's Bengal in India and as far northeast as Mongolia, the Tibetan Empire and China, starting in the 7th Century, often fought as each sought strategic advantage. As the empire weakened, Chinese imperialism began making inroads in Tibet. Chinese claims of sovereignty in Tibet date from 1727 when two Chinese representatives were posted there. However, exercise of Chinese sovereignty has been sporadic due to the vicissitudes of Chinese domestic politics. After the defeat of the Chinese in the Sino-Japanese War of 1895, Chinese sovereignty existed in name only. Chiang Kai-shek's Republic of China was too weak internally, too damaged by the Pacific and ensuing Civil Wars to ever give much attention to Tibet.

In 1950, shortly after the founding of the People's Republic of China (PRC), the People's Liberation Army (PLA) marched into the Chamdo area of Tibet and easily subdued the poorly armed Tibetan Army. In 1951, Tibetan representatives in Beijing were presented with the Seventeen Point Agreement (SPA), which declared China's sovereignty over Tibet. After a few months, the "agreement" was ratified in Lhasa. In violation of the SPA, China sought to remold Tibet's social and religious systems. Parts of Tibet, Eastern Kham and Amdo, were made parts of Sichuan and Qinghai Provinces, respectively. Land reform was carried out, accompanied by "struggle sessions," exposing landlords and supposed landlords to mass public humiliation.

As insensitive to Tibetan culture as China was, it did abolish slavery and serfdom, built highways, and subsidized the Tibetan government. However, it continued to increase control over lamas and fully instituted land reform, which led to rebellion in Eastern Kham and Amdo. Soon the rebellion spread to Western Kham and U-Tsang. In other parts of Tibet, China tried to create rural communes, just as it was doing in China proper, only to be met with resentment. China decided that the rebellion had gone too far and sent in the PLA to quell the rebels, which led to the "Lhasa Uprising" and Tibet-wide revolt. Concerned that the Dalai Lama might be arrested, Tibetans and the CIA helped the spiritual and political leader to escape to India.

In 1965, Tibet was officially made an "Autonomous Region" of the PRC with the provision that the head of government would be an ethnic Tibetan; however, the real power is in the hands of the Chinese Communist Party Secretary who has always been a Han Chinese with little experience, if any, in Tibet. The same holds true for the head of Public Security Bureau (police).

Interestingly, the General Secretary of the Chinese Communist Party, President of the PRC, and Chairman of the Military Control Commission Hu Jintao served as First Secretary of the Tibetan CCP in the late 80s. During Hu's watch, the second most important Tibetan religious figure, the Panchen Lama, who had the authority to select a new Dalai Lama, mysteriously died. Many Tibetans believe Hu was involved although it remains to be proven. However, national leaders in Beijing were so impressed by his handling of Tibet that he was summoned to Beijing where he was put on the fast track to the highest levels of Chinese national leadership.

William E. Sharp, Jr.

Chapter Four

TAIWAN

Taiwan: Overlooked and Underappreciated
Honolulu, November 12, 2006

Tobacco leaf shaped Taiwan is often overlooked and underappreciated due to the extensive coverage of China's economic development and growing presence on the international stage. However, Taiwan has achieved a higher level of overall development than China. Thus, it has valuable lessons to share with developing nations throughout the world in economic development, democratization, and public health.

Upon the Allied victory in World War II, Taiwan was liberated from Japanese colonial control and returned to the control of the Nationalist Chinese government, which dominated the Republic of China (ROC). At the time of reversion, Taiwan was mainly a large rice paddy that benefited from some good basic infrastructure in the form of railways and harbors that the Japanese had built during their fifty years of colonial control.

It became obvious that the Nationalist Chinese were unable to gain traction in the Chinese Civil War from 1945 to 1949. With the victory of the Chinese

Communists imminent, the nationalist government and two million supporters retreated to Taiwan where they reestablished the ROC.

With U.S. prodding, the Nationalists began to realize their shortcomings on the mainland which hastened their downfall. Pearl Buck's 1937 Pulitzer Prize winning novel, the *Great Earth* vividly portrayed the importance of owning land in the Chinese psyche and that land ownership was a key to acquiring wealth. Unfortunately, the lion's share of Chinese mainland landownership was concentrated in the hands of a small landowning class. Those that worked the land entered into usurious sharecropper arrangements with landlords to eke out an existence. To make matters worse, the landlords were a key pillar of Nationalist political support.

The Nationalist Government owed no similar allegiance to Taiwan landlords. Moreover, the success of the U.S. and South Korean authorities in carrying out land reform in South Korea from 1945 to 1950, and in Japan from 1946 to 1950 were impressive and gave hope that it could be repeated with success in Taiwan. With U.S. advice and assistance, between 1949 and 1953, land rents were first reduced and ultimately large landholders were compelled to sell their land at a fair price. The land was then sold to former sharecroppers at reasonable rates, which could be financed over a ten-year period.

By 1953, 80% of all arable land in Taiwan was owned by those who tilled it. Working their own land, agricultural production exploded and created a surplus that was exported to gain hard currency. Farming families' material lives began to steadily improve. Former landlords took their compensation and invested in Taiwan's nascent industrial base. With a vibrant agricultural sector and sizzling industrial growth, Taiwan created a firm economic base to which its economic success soon spoke for itself.

I first went to Taiwan in 1973 to study Chinese at Taiwan Normal University's Mandarin Training Center. In those days, Taiwan was clearly under a dictatorship exercising firm martial law. Local elections were tightly controlled, and no party other than the ruling Kuomintang (KMT) could legally campaign, although individuals could throw their hat into the ring. The National Assembly (NA), whose members had mainly been in office since being elected in the mainland, ostensibly elected the President and Vice-President. Since the ROC's authority was then only limited to Taiwan, NA members had a safe job until the ROC returned to the mainland where new elections to the body would be held. So the rationale went.

Chiang Ching-kuo (son of Chiang Kai-shek) became President of the ROC in 1978. In 1987, he lifted martial law which ushered in direct popular elections for President and Vice-President. Moreover, he allowed the formation of opposition parties that would be able to campaign on an equal basis with the Nationalist Party. Before these reforms were implemented, those who vigorously protested or demonstrated against the government were often arrested and prosecuted in a military court on sedition charges. Upon sentencing, they were sent off to Green Island, a small island off of the southeast corner of Taiwan to serve their time in a special prison for political prisoners. Today, the prison is a museum to remind people of the past.

There was no real legislative body where policy options could be debated. Owing to the growth of political parties in Taiwan, political life is very active, typified by the highly energetic "lifayuan" (legislature), which is often a stage for spirited debate that sometimes spills over into open brawls. People in Taiwan feel embarrassed about such antics. However, when the Japanese Diet first began to convene after World War II, in contemporarily democratized South Korea, and in the early days of the U.S., fist-fighting was a common practice in legislative bodies. It was just part of democratic maturation.

The large scale demonstrations carried out by former Democratic Progressive Party leader and founder, Shih Ming-teh's "red shirts" demanding President Chen Shui-bian's ouster in the lead up to the October 10 (Double Ten) National Day celebrations were further evidence of Taiwan's democratization. Claiming that the controversial Chen government was corrupt because of his son-in-law's arrest for insider trading and his wife's, Wu Shu-chen, acceptance of $100,000 dollars in vouchers for political favors from upscale Sogo Department Store, for which she was later cleared, the streets of Taipei and other cities swelled with red shirt clad demonstrators demanding Chen "xiatai" (step down). Not to be outdone, Chen's supporters the "pan-green" (green is the color of Chen's party, the DPP), would counter-demonstrate. The number of demonstrators varied depending on who was demonstrating and when, but ran as high as 200,000.

As a government invited member of an international group of journalists, I observed the October 10 National Day celebrations in front of the President's office in central Taipei. A number of parliament members in attendance doffed their outer wear to expose their red shirts, disrupting the events and demanding the President pack up and leave. Many Taiwanese government officials and political personalities were concerned that such demonstration would be embarrassing for Taiwan, especially in the eyes of the international community. Compared to the Taiwan of 1973 that I witnessed, I was impressed by the degree of democratic sophistication that Taiwan has gained. The security officials and police handled the situation with obvious sensitivity. Such would not have been the case in 1973 during Chiang Kai-shek's day or in today's mainland China where police are universally reviled. The police would have quickly resorted to violence in the form of punching and kicking to control demonstrators.

On November 3, another shoe dropped. Mrs. Chen and three aides were indicted by the Taiwan High Prosecutor's Office for embezzlement, forgery, and perjury, including falsifying $450,000 in receipts which she presented to the President's Office for reimbursement from a Presidential discretionary fund for secret diplomacy. President Chen directed his aides to make payment. However, Chen was not indicted, although he was clearly implicated, owing to Presidential immunity until his term expires in May 2008. On November 5 (Taiwan time), President Chen publicly stated that if his wife is found guilty that he would resign. It's unthinkable that any prosecutor would ever have even hinted that the elder Chiang or wife Soong Mei-ling might have crossed an unacceptable legal threshold. Public criticism of a key leader in mainland China spells incarceration.

As a leading global trading power, Taiwan's membership in the World Trade Organization (WTO) and the Asia-Pacific Economic Cooperation (APEC) is of obvious benefit to member countries. Owing to mainland China's policy that seeks to isolate Taiwan within Asia and the world at large, Taiwan's membership in the World Health Organization (WHO) has been blocked. Nevertheless, according to Dr. Lee Ming-liang, former ROC Health Minister, Taiwan's high level of medical care, medical professionalism, medical technology, research work on Hepatitis B, and readiness to confront Avian Flu, would make it a valuable member with much to share with all WHO members. Moreover, Taiwan has dispatched hundreds of health workers to developing countries and established curricula in Taiwan to train international public health workers. Taiwan's membership in the WHO would remove an obvious hole in the world wide health network resulting in more timely transmission and exchange of crucial health data.

In economics, politics, and public health, Taiwan has much to be proud of and much to share with the world. As its most steadfast supporter, the U.S. should also feel pride in Taiwan's successes.

U.S. Needs a Strong Taiwan
Honolulu, February 28, 2010

The Obama administration should be given credit for concluding a lingering Bush era arms sale to Taiwan and not yielding to China's insistence to stop all sales.

Relations between the U.S. and Taiwan are governed by the Taiwan Relations Act, which was passed by the Congress and signed by President Carter in 1979. A key provision of the act enables the U.S. to sell Taiwan defensive weapons.

Asian countries seek good economic and political relations with China; however, they closely observe how America conducts its relationship with Taiwan. How America deals with its longtime friend, Taiwan, is seen as an index of their own relations with the U.S. and just how committed the Obama administration is to re-engaging the region after the neglect shown during the administration of George W. Bush.

At one time or another, every country in Asia with which the U.S. has had a meaningful relationship has worried about abandonment. Secretary of State Hillary Clinton's cry, "We're back!" still has not convinced everyone.

It is clear that since Ma Ying-jeou assumed the Taiwan presidency in May 2008, cross-strait tensions have eased. However, the ultimate goals of the two sides differ considerably: Taiwan wants the economic benefits of a closer relationship while maintaining political separation from China; China seeks to use better economic relations with Taiwan as a tool to achieve political unification.

Viewed from another perspective, China seeks to use the ongoing Economic Cooperation Framework Agreement negotiations to increase Taiwan's economic dependence on China. At the same time, it uses its economic and political influence to dissuade other countries from negotiating free trade agreements with Taiwan or selling Taipei any weapons.

Militarily, Beijing seeks to intimidate Taiwan by failing to remove any of the reported 1,200 to 1,400 missiles aimed at Taiwan.

Selling defensive weapons to Taiwan helps to strengthen the Taiwanese military, plus it boosts Taiwan's self-confidence and morale. In the event of a mainland attack, Taiwan would need to hold the Chinese military at bay until American forces could arrive. A stronger Taiwan military reduces pressure on the U.S. and can make China realize that any attack on Taiwan could exact a human and material cost on China.

Providing defensive weapons to Taiwan under the framework of the Taiwan Relations Act enhances regional stability, a key goal of our East Asia policy.

To those who say the sale of weapons to Taiwan will hurt U.S.-China relations, one has to wonder just how helpful China has really been in stopping North Korean nuclear development.

China's primary goal in North Korea is to see a stable government, period.

Due to its demand for Iranian oil, China has been of little help in stemming Iranian nuclear development. It's increasingly clear that China wants to be the pre-eminent power in East Asia and would prefer that the U.S. leave the region.

Given its unremitting military buildup and penchant for secrecy, those in the American military who seek greater Chinese transparency are unlikely to gain much.

Others say that we have to consider the leverage in China's holdings of U.S. debt. In a recent East-West Wire, edited by the East-West Center, noted China scholar Kenneth Lieberthal said, "China only holds less than 7 percent of outstanding Treasury bills and less than 7 percent of Fannie Mae and Freddie Mac debt." Not the overwhelming amount that most assume.

Due to differences in the political systems and world views of the U.S. and China, problems will still remain in the relationship even if the "Taiwan problem" ceased to exist.

Upholding America's commitments to Taiwan is in the nation's best interest, despite China's protest.

Chen Shui-bian's Swan Song
Honolulu, February 8, 2010

The January 12, 2008 rout of the Democratic Progressive Party (DPP) in Taiwan's legislative elections brought to an end the era of President Chen Shui-bian. Doubling as DPP Chair, his influence permeated all aspects of the race. To his credit, he quickly tendered his resignation as chair once the disastrous results were clear. "It's the worst defeat the party suffered since its founding," said Chen.

Chen himself had advocated the electoral reform upon which the elections was held in hope of creating a more stable two-party system with better qualified candidates and a legislature that would function more smoothly. He got what he wanted: an election system based on seventy-three single member district seats, thirty-four seats based on proportional representation, and six seats to provide for aboriginal representation. Each voter cast two ballots: one for the candidate of their choice and one for the party of their choice.

Previous elections were held on the basis of 29 multi-member districts to fill 225 seats. It was reasonably easy to get elected in such a system and only required getting 4 to 5 percent of the total number of ballots cast. Even then, vote buying was not unheard of. Candidates were generally thought to be poorly qualified for legislative duties and often sounded sonorous, divisive campaign themes, which often focused on Taiwan independence as a quick fix to enhance electability. Such tactics often reappeared on the floor of the legislature and periodically devolved into open brawls, which Taiwan voters considered embarrassing.

Chen should have seen the writing on the wall. For the first time in the 2005 Local Elections comprised of county magistrates, county councilmen, and township governors, single member districts were used in place of multi-member districts. The local level was a one time political stronghold of the DPP where many party leaders (such as Vice-President Annette Lu and former Premier Su Tseng-chang) had launched their elected political careers. As a result of the change plus salient charges of corruption, the Nationalist Party (NP) took control of 16 of the 23 counties to become the dominant local level political party.

With new local level influence, the NP built a reputation of strong constituent service and erected an effective grass roots network to launch its highly successful "get out the vote" effort on January 12.

Considered to be one of the richest political parties in the world, the Nationalist Party, known as the Kuomintang (KMT), had large residual wealth, which was also helpful.

The formation of the new single member districts favored the KMT. Even under the multi-member district system, the NP candidate normally received the largest number of votes. Chen hoped to win 50 seats for the DPP. He only won 27 compared to the KMT's 81. The Non-Partisan Solidarity Union won three seats, the People First Party and an independent won one seat each.

The DPP's system of selecting candidates undoubtedly cost the party seats. To be crowned a candidate required one to adhere to an unyielding, dogmatic position favoring Taiwan independence. Candidates that were ideologically pure got the nod despite having little chance of winning. For example, Ms. Hsiao Bi-khim was Chair of the Legislature's Foreign Relations Committee, and helped to create a positive international image for Taiwan by taking a more balanced view of Taiwanese independence. If she had ran in Taipei City, District 2 (Shihlin-Datong), the DPP would likely have gained a seat since her would-be NP opponent, and the ultimate winner of the election, was considered quite weak.

Throughout his nearly eight years in office, Chen was obsessed with crafting a new cultural and political identity for the people of Taiwan and bringing about *de jure* independence. He lost touch with the Taiwan man on the street who was generally far more interested in buoying up Taiwan's sagging economy, which was experiencing the lowest growth rate in a group of 20 Asian economies. The DPP lacked concrete proposals on re-energizing the economy and economic talent. Post election analysis showed that the DPP lost influence with independent voters and the young voter who had enthusiastically supported the party. Chen further alarmed the electorate by impairing relations with America, upon whose security shield Taiwan ultimately depends, and risking further tension in relations with China. There is little wonder that the NP secured 53% of the vote, while the DPP only got 38.2%.

Does this mean that NP presidential candidate Ma Ying-jeou was a shoo-in for President in the March 22, 2008, Presidential election? Perhaps. Ma was cleared of corruption charges, and, despite the unreliability of Taiwan political opinion polls, seemed to be gathering momentum. On the other hand, voter turnout promised to be higher during the Presidential election and to favor the DPP. Taiwan voters are said to want a division of power and would be uncomfortable with both the Presidency and legislature under the control of any one party. This is especially so in the case of the NP; many still vividly recalled the KMT's abuse of power during Taiwan's pre-democratic era.

The challenge for both Ma and his DPP opponent, former Premier and Kaohsiung Mayor Frank Hsieh was to maneuver Taiwan back into its nebulous status quo, which would allow it to concentrate on economic development, repair relations with America, ease internal worry about unification with China, and alleviate China's concern about Taiwan seeking independence.

Ma's Taiwan
Taipei, Taiwan, August 10, 2008

Campaigning on the slogan: "No independence, no unification, no use of force," candidate Ma Ying-jeou hoped to recapture the President's Office for his

Kuomintang (KMT) party and to boost Taiwan's economy by more directly linking it to mainland China.

No sooner inaugurated on May 20, 2008, the Ma Administration was busy pursuing improved cross strait economic relations. To pump up Taiwan's tourist industry, three thousand mainland tourists per day for ten days were allowed into Taiwan. Large Taiwan companies were allowed to invest 60% of assets in mainland enterprises and mainland capital can be invested in Taiwan. Despite carrying out campaign promises, Ma's support in a United Daily News opinion poll slipped from 66% on May 20 to 50% on June 19. Many in the opposition Democratic Progressive Party (DPP) feared that Taiwan would be instantly united with the mainland. However, few stopped to realize that the DPP had conducted much of the negotiations to improve commercial relations with the mainland, but ran out of time in office before all of the finishing touches could be put in place. Thus, the KMT quickly took up where the DPP had left off. Moreover, those changes were long sought by both Taiwanese businessmen and the American Chamber of Commerce in Taiwan.

In June, news broke that the U.S. would not be providing sixty-six F-16 Cs and Ds the Taiwan government had repeatedly requested. Trying to determine just which side halted the deal was a matter for speculation. One prominent theory was that faced by a failing presidency, President Bush was trying to salvage some sort of legacy. To do so, he didn't want to hurt relations with China whose help he needed in dealing with North Korea and Iran. Moreover, not supplying the combat aircraft would enhance stability in East Asia, a long-term, fundamental U.S. goal in the region.

The prominent explanation was that the Taiwan government actually wanted to suspend the deal. After all, on July 14, Taiwan's *Liberty Times* reported the Taiwan government dropped plans to upgrade the Indigenous Defense Fighter, one of the three main types of combat aircraft in the Republic of China Air Force. According to Dr. Andrew Yang, Secretary General of the Chinese Council of Advanced Policy Studies, "75% of the people in Taiwan do not think that China will attack the island." That being the case, why worry about arms purchases? By foregoing the F-16s, Ma could be hoping to create momentum for a peace treaty with China that could result in the removal of the eleven to fourteen hundred missiles in Taiwan aimed at Taiwan. Or, he might be seeking China's good will in preparation for Taiwan's application to the UN.

Speaking at a mid-July forum of the Heritage Foundation, in Washington, D.C., Admiral Timothy Keating, Pacific Commander of U.S. Forces, confirmed that there was a freeze on arms sales to Taiwan, calling the decision "administration policy." Officials who made the decision "reconciled Taiwan's military posture, China's current military posture and strategy that indicates there is no pressing, compelling need for, at this moment, arms sales to Taiwan." However, a mere four months before, at the time of the Taiwan presidential election in March, the U.S. deployed two aircraft carriers, the Kitty Hawk and Nimitz, to waters close to Taiwan to prevent People's Republic of China harassment of the island.

Randy Schriver, former Deputy Assistant Secretary of State for East Asian and Pacific Affairs in the current Bush administration, co-authored a strongly worded July 19 *Wall Street Journal* op-ed calling for the resumption of arms sales to Taiwan. Schriver wrote that to deny the weapons to Taiwan would be to undercut its negotiating position, and simply put more pressure on the U.S. military to respond in the event of an emergency since Taiwan would be less capable of defending itself. Taiwan is a long-term democratic friend, and the way the U.S. handled this situation reflects on its image throughout the region. Vice-Admiral Lang Ning-li, retired Chief of Taiwan Naval Intelligence and a researcher at the National Policy Foundation pointed out, "Air defense and anti-submarine warfare are crucial to Taiwan's defense."

The F-16 Cs and Ds might never be delivered to Taiwan. Their advanced design and ability to deliver cruise missiles casts them as an offensive weapon, while the U.S. prefers to supply Taiwan with defensive weapons only, despite obvious mainland advantages in missile weaponry. However, according to Taiwan Business Council Chair, and former World Bank President and Deputy Assistant Secretary of Defense, Paul Wolfowitz, another important weapons package will be delivered that calls for a feasibility study of the U.S. building eight submarines for Taiwan, thirty Apache helicopters, sixty Black Hawk helicopters, spare parts for

F-16s, and Patriot III anti-missile missiles.

The Kuomintang (KMT) is in a seemingly enviable position controlling the Presidency, the legislature, and most county magistrate and city mayor positions. However, 40% of the population still voted for the Democratic Progress Party (DPP) in the presidential election. The KMT is not a monolith, and Ma was not a strong leader. In the parlance of the KMT, Ma was "light blue" or somewhat of a liberal within the party as compared to the "dark blue" or conservative wing of the party. Because he tried to reach out and appoint people with previous DPP connections to the Control Yuan and Executive Yuan, he could not consolidate his party's support and had to withdraw the nominations.

Taiwan is a burgeoning democratic society. As such, Taiwan has the only stable and viable two-party democratic system in Northeast Asia. Japan has a one and one-half party system where except for a very short period of time the Liberal Democratic Party has been in control. The fluid party system in South Korea sees parties appear and then disappear. Whether Taiwan will remain a two-party system is open to question. The legislative elections held in January under the new single member district system reduced the DPP to only 27 seats in the 113 seat chamber.

Led by former President Chen Shui-bian, eight years of DPP rule deepened Taiwan's democracy, made significant improvements in infrastructure, and passed important social legislation, said Soochow University political scientist Dr. Lo Chih-cheng. Nevertheless, the

DPP's legacy is tarnished. Chen, his wife, former Vice-President Annette Lu, and five of his ministers have been indicted for corruption.

DPP insiders feel there is little chance that they can make a comeback in the 2012 legislative elections, claiming that the electoral districts favor the KMT. Fielding electable presidential candidates is challenging in that the old guard is pretty much discredited, and it is hard to find anyone under fifty-five with the enthusiasm, energy, and ability to focus on economic issues, rather than persistently calling for independence. According to a Mainland Affairs Council poll conducted in March, 90% of Taiwanese support the status quo. Gains might be made in county magistrate and mayoral elections, but as the KMT proved, its strong local connections built during the long period of martial law are still paying off today. The KMT is considered one of the wealthiest political parties in the world; the DPP has yet to organize an effective fund raising strategy.

Ma needs to carry out the *rapprochement* with the Mainland and the disposition of Chen in a manner that consolidates popular support. Even given the economic benefits, too rapid or extensive an engagement with the Mainland has the potential to bring thousands of protesters onto the streets of Taiwan, reminiscent of the 2006 Red Shirt movement seeking to force Chen from office. Despite liberalization in cross-straits relations, it is almost certain that China will block Taiwan's sixteenth attempt to rejoin the UN this fall. As a result, Ma and the KMT could lose support. If not carefully handled, the manner in which Ma deals with the indictment, prosecution, and possible sentencing of Chen could create major upheaval.

Playing the Taiwan Issue for Party Unity
Honolulu, October 14, 2007

Approaching Taiwan's January 2008 parliamentary elections and the March 2008 Presidential election plus the opening next week of China's 17th National Party Congress, political leaders on both sides of the Taiwan Strait are manipulating the issue of Taiwan's future political status to promote the benefit of the Democratic Democratic Progressive Party (DPP) in Taiwan and the Chinese Communist Party (CCP) in China.

Taiwan President Chen Sui-bian never promised he would end his presidency quietly. A master at brinksmanship, it would be completely out of character for him not to continue promoting Taiwan independence in his unrelenting quest for international recognition of Taiwan's political sovereignty.

Despite more popular concern for economic growth than for Taiwan's independence, spotty diplomatic support from the mere 24 nations that do maintain relations with Taiwan, being rejected for admission to the World Health Organization ten times and just having suffered its fifteenth rejection for admission to the UN, Chen still persists in his crusade for international respect and to end what he calls "Taiwan's humiliation" orchestrated by China.

In the wake of such setbacks, Chen is promoting a referendum on Taiwan's admission to the UN as "Taiwan" rather than the "Republic of China" to be voted on at the same time as the presidential election. Such a stratagem has unsurprisingly brought protest and military threats from China who see it as a way of further distancing Taiwan from China. Moreover, it has contributed to a deteriorating relationship between Taiwan and its principal benefactor, the U.S.

The U.S.'s primary goal in East Asia is to preserve political stability. The U.S. does not maintain formal diplomatic relations with Taiwan, but it is bound by the Taiwan Relations Act, which gives the U.S. the option of coming to Taiwan's defense in the event of a Chinese military attack. However, Chen risks the stability of East Asia and abuses the relationship with the U.S. by continuing to push the sovereignty issue and provoking China, assuming that any Chinese military response he may trigger will automatically be met by a U.S. military response.

Politically, the U.S. position is that the future of Taiwan must be worked out cooperatively between Taiwan and mainland China, thus pre-empting a unilateral action on behalf of either party.

The parliamentary and presidential elections represent both challenge and opportunity for Chen's Democratic Progressive Party (DPP). During his two terms, Chen's and the DPP's success have been hampered by Nationalist

Party (NP) control of the legislature. The parliamentary election will be the first time representatives are selected from single member districts rather than multiple member districts. The number of representatives will be cut from 225 to 113. Many feel the party that scores the first victory in the reformed system will gain long-term electoral benefit.

The March 2008 presidential election will also likely be very close. The NP will not be divided such as it was when James Soong bolted the party in 2000 to create his People First Party and opened the path to Chen's first term. In 2004, Chen won by less than a percentage point only after a suspicious assassination attempt on him and Vice President Lu Hsiu-lien.

Chen supported former Premier Su Tseng-chang as his heir apparent. However, Su lost to Frank Hsieh (Hsieh Chang-ting) in the intra-party primary. By all accounts, Hsieh, also a former premier and former mayor of Kaohsiung, is more pragmatic and less zealous about Taiwan independence than Chen. He also realizes that taking an extreme position on Taiwan independence would cost him support with more moderate voters.

Nevertheless, Chen has promised to be very active in the presidential campaign, and through his machinations, Su is on the DPP ballot as vice president. Hsieh would have preferred former Minister of Transportation and Communications, the widowed Yeh Chu-lan. "I also think there is growing concern that Chen is trying to box in his successor, to force the next president to continue his policies," said a leading Taiwan specialist, Shelley Rigger of Davidson College in North Carolina.

Rigger is right. On October 3, the DPP Central Standing Committee selected Chen as its new chairman. He will have great influence over both the legislative and presidential elections, and whether the DPP's tenure and his policies will continue. Hsieh will need Chen's help and be forced to accommodate him more than he otherwise might wish.

Fully appreciating how close the elections could likely be, Chen's posturing on the UN referendum is more geared to rallying the DPP's base to ensure victory in both parliamentary and presidential elections, rather than actually winning international recognition for Taiwan. Playing such a role can also help to secure his place in Taiwan's history and to defend against corruption charges facing him, his wife, family members, and certain staff members.

Across the Taiwan Strait in China, the run up to the 17th National Party Congress has been especially contentious. As China continues to economically develop, different schools of political thought evolve within the CCP, creating greater factionalism. Thus, deciding how many seats on the Politburo Standing Committee and full Politburo to allocate to which faction and in what person has been an especially difficult task. This is all the more sensitive when considering the role of Shanghai Clique members whose careers were promoted by the still powerful former CCP General Secretary, Jiang Zemin, a political opponent of the current General Secretary Hu Jintao.

All of this comes on top of the March National People's Congress which was preceded by fiery public outcry about passage of the Private Property Protection Law (Wuquanfa). The PPL was first introduced in 2002 but could not be passed until just this year due to a lack of popular support and consensus among representatives. Despite ultimate passage of the law, the session was not without dissent. Statements by Premier Wen Jiabao emphasizing Chinese sovereignty over Taiwan and the threat of military force to pre-empt any attempt to sever Taiwan from the mainland brought instant unity and howling support from all representatives.

Statements made in recent weeks and on China's National Day, October 1, by key members of China's national leadership indicate that Taiwan will be a key agenda item that will receive much attention at the party congress. Given the emotive and unifying impact of the mention of Taiwan in mainland China, discussion about Taiwan will be geared to promoting party unity.

Taiwan's political future remains unclear. Nevertheless, rhetoric about Taiwan's sovereignty is a proven way to elicit political support in both Taipei and Beijing.

Taiwan Under Leveraging Resources
Honolulu, February 8, 2009

Thank heaven and thank earth, as the Chinese

expression goes, tensions across the Taiwan Strait have subsided during the first eight months of the Ma Ying-jeou presidency. Nevertheless, one wonders if Taiwan is leveraging its substantial resources to its greatest advantage or rushing into a false sense of greater economic dependence on the mainland while China ignores Taiwan's sovereignty.

With investments totaling nearly $150 billion, Taiwan is the largest investor in China. There are an estimated fifty thousand Taiwan businesses in the mainland where one million business people and their families reside.

The Pearl River Delta is often considered the epicenter of China's export based economy. According to Max Hirsch, writing for the Kyodo News Service, "Taiwan holds the key to preventing Southern China's industrial base from flying off the rails."

In Central China, Taiwan investment is playing a leading role in transforming Wuhan into a modern industrial base, logistics center, and transportation hub. According to People's Republic of China, Ministry of Commerce statistics, Taiwan investment in Wuhan totals $2.42 billion. In addition, Taiwan's Foxconn Corporation plans to make Wuhan the digital camera production center of the world, which will create 200,000 jobs.

A hallmark of the Hu Jintao and Wen Jiabao stewardship of China has been the development of Tianjin as a modern port facility and services center in Northern China. Joining in the effort has been over two thousand Taiwan enterprises. In December 2008, Taiwan businesses decided to invest an additional $2.9 billion in

Tianjin, bringing total Taiwan investment in the northern city to $8.2 billion.

Taiwan business in China gives China access to needed technology and managerial expertise. Despite China's obvious success in foreign trade, it still lacks the savvy to crack certain markets that Taiwan has acquired much experience in over its longer period of involvement in the global economy.

Inexplicably, the ruling Nationalist Party (NP) seems to underrate Taiwan's bargaining chips when negotiating with China, preferring to exaggerate any agreement as a major breakthrough. Interestingly, most of the negotiating for this new connectivity was done by the Democratic Progressive Party (DPP) while still in power, leaving the NP to put on the finishing touches.

It's too early to assess what long-term successes might come from greater interaction between Taiwan and China. Increased mainland tourism was promoted as a panacea to Taiwan's tepid service industry but has not lived up to expectations. Chinese investment in the Taiwan stock market, banks, and real estate has yet to concretize. Charter flights, direct flights, plus direct sea and air cargo have all begun. Such transportation links could help increase Taiwan bound tourism and allow business people from both sides to move back and forth across the strait less expensively and more quickly. Ma Ying-jeou has sought to de-emphasize the role of the military in cross strait relations; however, China has only offered vague promises of removing any of the 1,100 to 1,400 missiles it has aimed at Taiwan.

Taiwan has long sought added "international space" or visibility on the global stage. Despite the rapprochement in Taiwan-China relations, the island's application for observer status in the World Health Organization was blocked by China. Instead, it will be granted membership in the global health alert system. China continues to block Taiwan's participation in the Association of Southeast Asian Nations as a dialogue partner despite the economic advantages Taiwan can offer to the region.

From the perspective of pure economic benefit, this might not be the right time for Taiwan to determinedly seek to tie its economic future to China. Since 1978, the Chinese economy has grown at nearly 10% a year. The International Monetary Fund predicts that it will only grow at half that rate this year. Exports will be off 6% this year, according to the Fitch Report. According to the Chinese Academy of Social Sciences, unemployment will rise to 9%, although many predict the rate will actually be much higher in that the academy's prediction does not take into account the 200 million migrant workers who have been the backbone of China's economic development.

Then, there is the question of just how deep pocketed China really is. It promulgated an economic stimulus program that it couldn't or wouldn't fully fund, is committed to financing improvements in rural life, rebuilding Southwest China after last spring's devastating natural disaster, and claimed it will take care of Southeast Asia and Hong Kong in the wake of further economic fallout. At the same time such commitments were being made, China was increasing its borrowing from abroad. According to the State Administration of Foreign Exchange, Chinese debt stands at $442 billion, which is an 18.3% increase over the total at the end of 2007.

China is likely to see a rash of civil unrest this year. In the spring, when the migrant workers return from their villages to the factory towns where they have worked and find abandoned or bankrupted factories (and thus no work), wide scale demonstration is likely to envelop the country. Moreover, this year's calendar is rife with anniversary and commemoration dates ideally suited for political protest: the 60th Anniversary of the founding of the People's Republic of China, the 20th Commemoration of the Tien An Men Incident, the 90th Anniversary of the May Fourth Movement, the 50th year since the Dalai Lama fled Tibet.

To help ward off social upheaval, there is an increase in use of Marxist rhetoric, urging of the public to obey the Chinese Communist Party, and ramped up discipline in the People's Liberation Army, the ultimate guarantor of stability. All of this comes from a party which in recent years has felt much more at home talking about the benefits of market economics, rather than spewing out political slogans.

The exact nature of their motivation remains unclear. Nevertheless, the pro-China wing of the NP led by one time presidential candidate Lien Chan, NP Party Chairman, Wu Po-hsiung, and James Soong, a former NP presidential aspirant who bolted the party to form his own People First Party, relentlessly rush on to create greater connectivity with China. The three seem to own the issue with Ma, exercising little discernible influence. Moreover, popular dismay exists due to the lack of transparency in which negotiations are being carried on between the NP and the Chinese Communist Party. Many, including Legislative President and NP member Wang Jyn-ping, would be more comfortable if relations were carried out with the support of the legislature. Others would prefer cross strait relations to be carried out on a government to government basis.

While better economic relations with China are desired, Taiwan's Mainland Affairs Council polling shows that only 4.8% of the population would consider unification with their cross strait neighbor at some undetermined future time, while 1.8 % want immediate unification.

Promoting Taiwan's Soft Power
Honolulu, September 1, 2010

The greatest benefit to Taiwan from the recently passed Economic Cooperation Framework Agreement will be to give Taiwan a greater ability to more freely maneuver on the international stage and to strike free trade agreements (FTAs).

To echo the realistic view of the *Economist*, the people of Taiwan will not unify with China simply to take advantage of a few tariff breaks or experience a permanent peace across the Taiwan Strait, especially as China has failed to reduce its missile arsenal aimed at Taiwan.

Achieving FTAs with Southeast Asian nations and beyond is crucial to President Ma Ying-jeou's re-election campaign. Therefore, if China pressures Southeast Asian nations not to sign FTAs with Taiwan, Ma's electoral hopes will be diminished. Such a result would not be in China's interest. China is comfortable with Ma and feels that they can trust him. Their worst nightmare is the return to power of the independence minded Democratic Progressive Party.

Between now and the 2012 presidential election, Taiwan has a window of opportunity to vigorously promote itself on the international stage to better economically connect itself to other countries. In turn, Taiwan's own identity and sovereignty will be strengthened.

To achieve such, Taiwan must seriously improve the promotion of its international image. To its detriment, Taiwan's global visibility is greatly overshadowed by China's and will remain so, unless there is some new, imaginative, out of the box thinking, and a halt to constantly fretting about China's reaction to any action Taiwan might take.

High-priced Taiwan government advertisements placed in upscale U.S. magazines seem to have limited effect in creating a clear image of Taiwan in the minds of many. Unfortunately, the mention of Taiwan to many

Americans elicits the response that the shopping in "Bangkok" (Thailand) is fantastic.

The challenge is here and now! The Taiwan Lobby in the U.S. Congress was weakened during the Chen Shui-bian-era. Now, China is implementing many of the Taiwan Lobby's successful techniques employed during its heyday. The growth in influence of the pro-China Business Lobby only adds to the urgency of the matter. While China aggressively expands the number of its Confucian Institutes, of which there are already 316 operating in 94 countries that serve as instruments of soft power through which it seeks to spread language study and influence, I have yet to see or hear of any promised Taiwan Academy being established.

As China prepares to mold world opinion with its widely expanded information campaign, Taiwan ought to follow the example of Japan or Germany. Japan's *NHK World* is an English language TV program that is broadcast in U.S. and focuses on Japanese affairs. Germany enhances its global image through the *Deutsche Welle,* which broadcasts TV shows, in a wide variety of languages, about all aspects of contemporary Germany. Other examples can be found in the *BBC World News* and *France 24*. Clearly, China sees the benefit of such TV programs as it will soon start its own English language TV programming with global reach.

During a recent visit to the East-West Center in Hawaii, eminent U.S. China scholar Jerome Cohen said it all, "It [Taiwan] is certainly free and certainly impressive. Taiwan is a great product for soft power. It has something to sell," but hasn't made enough effort to get its story out. It is the story of an agrarian based one time colony that bore the brunt of authoritarianism under the boot of martial law and transformed itself into a key link in the global supply chain of computer parts and a vibrant participatory democracy based on the rule of law. Many nations would like to enjoy the standard of living and freedom that Taiwan has achieved.

Taiwan's priorities are confused. Suffering a dismal showing in the 2008 Olympics, Taiwan is reported to be investing significantly increased sums in creating a more competitive 2012 Olympic team without fear of angering China. At the same time, it seems to only be capable of hand wringing when it comes to improving international communications.

The TRA and Taiwan's Democracy
Taipei, Taiwan, May 3, 2009

April 2009 marked the 30th anniversary of the Taiwan Relations Act (TRA), one of the most successful pieces of legislation in the history of U.S. foreign policy.

The TRA provides the stability for Taiwan and Asia to economically develop. It also supports the security of Taiwan by enabling the U.S., upon consultation between the president and Congress, to sell defensive weapons to Taiwan and come to Taiwan's defense.

U.S. Congressional bipartisan support appears to

remain strong for the TRA, and the Obama White House will continue support for the island. The TRA also has provided the security for the Taiwan government to ease tensions with mainland China, something that is welcome across the board.

However, there is a growing military imbalance between the two parties, which could threaten this new sense of peacefulness, according to former U.S. Ambassador to China, Winston Lord.

China's military budget has repeatedly increased by double-digit figures in recent years, and China still maintains as many as 1,400 missiles aimed at Taiwan. On the other hand, Taiwan's military is experiencing a budget cut, reduced quality in training, and aging of its combat aircraft—all while downsizing to an all-volunteer force targeted at approximately 250,000. China's People's Liberation Army has 2.3 million under arms.

The key to maintaining a high level of U.S. congressional and popular support for Taiwan is the continual refinement of its democracy. With freedom of speech, popular election of public officials, and Asia's most developed two-party system, Taiwan is a highly successful example of how a once-authoritarian state can transform into a vibrant democracy.

Nevertheless, concern is growing about the polarization of Taiwan society and the growing frequency with which those in Taiwan refer to their society as an "M" society—one with a diminishing middle class, a growing number of poor, and a certain number of wealthy who are becoming wealthier.

Politically, Taiwan is more polarized between the opposition Democratic Progressive Party (DPP) and the ruling Kuomintang (KMT). There is a lack of a political center in Taiwan. Simply put, the DPP does not support rapprochement with the mainland for fear that Taiwan will lose its sovereignty and hope for future *de jure* independence; the KMT supports eventual unification with mainland China and is actively promoting further economic integration.

This disparity has led to large-scale DPP street demonstrations, with more promised. Political observers in Taiwan are especially concerned about this, given the civil unrest gripping Thailand. Fortunately, owing to the democratization of the military since 1989, even the most anti-government observers discount the possibility of military intervention into politics.

Given the disarray, one wonders if Taiwan will remain a viable two-party system. The KMT controls the presidency, the legislature, and most local government positions. A despondent key DPP insider said that if the party retains the six local government positions it now holds in the upcoming local elections, it will be doing well.

The party is plagued by a lack of finances and the lingering negative image of former president and DPP chairman Chen Shui-bian, who is in jail facing corruption charges. Moreover, the party lacks a center of gravity because of the strong factionalism between the more pragmatic wing of the party versus the strongly doctrinaire pro-Taiwan independence wing of the party.

"Taidu" (Taiwan independence) has no chance of succeeding in the near future, and as long as those advocating that position within the party persist, the DPP will remain out of power. The DPP needs to focus more on economic issues and transform itself into a British-style labor party, which represents the interests of those economically less fortunate.

Revamping U.S.-Taiwan Relations
Honolulu, March 9, 2008

Should the U.S.-Taiwan relationship be managed as an appendage of U.S.-China relations? Or, should it be managed as a separate bilateral relationship? The report, *Strengthen Freedom in Asia: A Twenty-First Century Agenda for the U.S.-Taiwan Partnership* written by the American Enterprise Institute (AEI) for Public Policy Research and Armitage International, supports the latter approach reflecting the view of Washington's "pan-Asian faction" that U.S. Asian policy is strengthened by emphasizing alliances. The so-called "old China hands" faction advocates that all U.S. relations in Asia be worked out through the U.S.-China relationship.

The *AEI-Armitage Report* sees Taiwan as a free, democratic, prosperous, and strong society, which is in the U.S. interest to see continue. In just a very short time span of less than sixty years, it has gone from rags to riches and dictatorship to democracy.

America's fundamental foreign policy goal in East Asia is to preserve stability. China's military build up and positioning of over 1,000 missiles, 400,000 troops opposite Taiwan in Fujian Province and maintaining over 500 combat aircraft that can reach the island, presents a growing potential to alter the military balance of power, which has preserved both peace and stability in the Taiwan Strait.

The People's Republic of China (PRC) seeks to internationally isolate Taiwan and has prevailed upon the U.S. government to limit its official contacts with the island, not support its admission to the UN, and halt arms sales. China has also used its influence with large U.S. multi-national corporations investing in China to urge the U.S. government to distance itself from Taiwan. And to some degree has conditioned its pivotal role in the Six-Party Talks for flexibility in the U.S. position on Taiwan. The result has been for Taiwan to feel abandoned and to increase the shrill of its call for independence that only elicits threats of Chinese military force.

The continuation of such a pattern isn't in U.S. interests, and a more positive dialog needs to be immediately started with Taiwan that will lead to a more meaningful relationship, with Taiwan's participation in regional and international organizations such as the Association of Southeast Asian Nations and the World Health Organization. Taiwan has plenty of lessons and resources that it can share in economic and democratic development, provision of international aid, and promotion of higher global heath standards. However, to make such contributions, Taiwan has to be able to more actively participate in international affairs.

As the AEI and Armitage International see it, their proposal would stabilize the Taiwan Strait and help to secure American interests in a prosperous, stable Asia while not compromising standing U.S. policy. U.S. policy seeks to create a level playing field free of coercion that will facilitate dialog between the PRC and Taiwan.

Taiwan has definite economic credentials. Its economy surpasses that of Hong Kong and Singapore. The island plays a crucial role in the world hi-tech market, being the largest manufacturer of computer parts that supplies such U.S. computer companies as Apple, Dell, Hewlett-Packard, and Qualcomm. Astride the Taiwan Strait, a major sea lane, the port of Kaohsiung, in southern Taiwan, handles more containers than any single port in Japan or South Korea.

Taiwan elections are open and fair; moreover, civil and political liberties are zealously protected as attested to by the U.S. Department of State. As such, Taiwan is a model for other developing countries that are pursuing the establishment of democracy.

A one time beneficiary of U.S. foreign aid, Taiwan is now a provider of assistance in the South Pacific, Central America, South America, and Africa.

Taiwan has also been a solid player in countering the flow of narcotics, infectious disease, nuclear proliferation, and providing disaster relief.

Taiwan is a "responsible stakeholder," a term coined by former U.S. Deputy Secretary of State Robert B.

Zoellick to describe a role he suggested China play along with the U.S. and other nations in promoting a peaceful, stable international system.

Any one-sided, coerced "settlement" by the PRC to alter Taiwan's status would hurt U.S. strategic regional and international interests. American credibility would be severely tarnished, and its ability to play a leading role in East Asia as a stabilizing force would be seriously impaired. Moreover, PRC control of Taiwan would also give it a stage to further extend its influence into the Western Pacific, again at the expense of the U.S.

The *AEI-Armitage Report* comes in the midst of the final run-up to the Taiwan Presidential election on March 22, the U.S. Presidential election further down the road, and the opening of China's annual National People's Congress last week. Both Taiwan presidential candidates realize that Taiwan's relations with the U.S. have suffered and require immediate repair. U.S. Presidential candidates are primarily concerned with the Middle East and need to present a broader world view. Hard hitting statements about Chinese sovereignty over Taiwan are common fare in the National People's Congress and foster a sense of unity among representatives while eliciting uniformly deafening applause.

This year, Communist Party General Secretary and Chinese President, Hu Jintao, might have gone a step further by offering Taiwan the opportunity to engage in peace talks with the mainland on an equal basis (they acknowledged Chinese sovereignty based on the "one nation, two systems" notion). Taiwan rejected the offer given the condition, as it has consistently done in the past. At the same time China was offering peace talks, it announced a double digit increase in military spending for the nineteenth time; this time at the clip of 18% bringing the total officially acknowledged budget to $59 billion.

With their eyes on China, the winners of both Presidential elections will be the decisive factors in determining the course of U.S.-Taiwan relations.

William E. Sharp, Jr.

Chapter Five

KOREA

Lee Myung-bak's Korea
Honolulu, November 14, 2009

The keystone of Republic of Korea (ROK) President Lee Myung-bak's foreign policy is a strong strategic relationship with the U.S. The South Korean military is a highly respected fighting force, yet Korea ultimately relies on the U.S. security guarantee embodied in the ROK-U.S. Mutual Security Treaty.

Economically, Lee has lobbied for passage of the Korea-U.S. Free Trade Agreement (KORUSFTA) from the day he assumed the presidency. Studies have shown that passage would result in the U.S. economy growing by $10 billion annually and by 2018, Korea's would grow by 6%. U.S. resistance has come from the cattle industry that has encountered barriers in exporting beef to Korea, and the automobile industry that fears KORUSFTA will only add to the imbalance in the automobile trade between both countries. A compromise is clearly in the strategic and economic interests of both countries. ROK Ambassador to Washington Han Duck-soo predicted that the U.S. would ultimately pass the KORUSFTA in early

2010, after settlement of health care reform.

Lee's views on South Korean-Japan relationships are inspired. "I want a mature relationship with Japan," he said. More recently, he advocated that the focus of ROK relations with Japan should be on the future, not the past. Progress in the relationship is clear: Visiting Seoul on October 9, 2009, Japanese Prime Minister Hatoyama Yukio said that Lee's "grand bargain" to end North Korea's nuclear program was "absolutely correct." Lee's grand bargain promises massive aid for complete denuclearization. Lee gave equal support for Hatoyama's plan for an Asian regional organization built along the lines of the European Union.

There has been a cooling in Sino-South Korean relations. Soon after taking office, the Blue House (Korea's equivalent of the White House) resurrected the 1970s era Seoul-Tokyo-Washington triangle as a hedge against China. As Seoul saw it, China was either unwilling or unable to exert sufficient pressure on North Korea to abandon its nuclear weapons. China reasons that North Korea would never launch a nuclear missile in its direction. The possible collapse of North Korea and ensuing instability on the peninsula is of far greater worry to Beijing. In such a scenario, South Korean and U.S. troops would likely rush north to unify Korea under Seoul's control, denying China the buffer zone that now exists, and altering the geostrategic situation in Northeast Asia in a manner unacceptable to China.

Following the East Asian Economic Model with its emphasis on cheap labor to fuel export led economic growth, South Korea became a wealthy country. However, labor is no longer cheap, and South Korean labor unions are far from docile. Thus, manufacturing has had to move abroad to areas offering cheap unorganized labor, contributing to growing unemployment at home. Korea has to find a new model for continued economic growth and increased employment. Given the high cost of living and a growing number of Koreans living pay check to pay check, stimulating domestic demand doesn't seem like it could take the place of lost exports or jobs.

In fact, the *Korea Herald* said, "South Korea has experienced the fastest income polarization among the rich Organization for Economic Cooperation and Development nations over the past decade." Since the 1998 Asian Financial Crisis, the number of low-income people has increased due to a scarcity of jobs. At the same time, some of those with more financial assets could see them grow as a result of rising stock and real estate prices added onto their regular salaries.

To keep a manufacturing base and expand job opportunities, South Korea has to develop more value added high tech products. With greater innovation and added creativity, Korean manufacturing might be able to move away from the highly disciplined manufacturing it has become known for and move further into bio-engineering, environmental protection "Green" industries, or the aerospace industry where some work is now being done.

Another solution to Korea's economic malaise is to improve the foreign investment environment. According to a Korea Chamber of Commerce and Industry survey conducted among five hundred foreign firms, the Korean investment environment is behind that of Singapore, Hong Kong, and Taiwan in terms of incentive programs, deregulation efforts, and legal consistency. Lee clearly understands the situation and is trying to improve the investment environment. However, he is running into bureaucratic resistance.

One shouldn't forget how Korea first transformed itself from a poor backward country to a leading international economic power in a relatively short period of time, and how individual Korean citizens rallied to sell gold jewelry to help pay off International Monetary Fund loans ahead of schedule in order to minimize global shame. Recalling both feats, one feels confident that Korea will successfully deal with its contemporary problems.

ROK-U.S. Relations: Getting Back on Track
Honolulu, March 11, 2007

Based on shared security and economic concerns, Republic of Korea (ROK)-U.S. relations were especially strong between Korea's liberation from Japanese colonial rule in 1945 until the "Gwangju Massacre" in 1980. Since then, the relationship has been on far too long of a down swing.

Under the aegis of the United Nations Command, the

U.S. helped South Korea hold off the North Koreans and the Chinese during the Korean War of 1950-1953, at the cost of over 33,000 American lives. In 1954, the Korea-U.S. Mutual Defense Treaty was signed committing the U.S. to the defense of South Korea, where the U.S. still maintains 29,089 troops.

South Korea supported the U.S. in Vietnam by deploying a total of 50,000 troops, including its highly respected Tiger and White Horse Divisions that turned out to be the most feared of all coalition troops. Despite strain in the South Korea-U.S. relationship, the ROK sent 3,300 troops (later reduced to 2,300) to support the U.S. in Iraq, which is the third largest troop contribution of any country.

Economically, the U.S. worked with South Korean authorities to carry out the land reform of 1945-1950, which created a more equitable economic base, stabilizing the country for future industrialization. South Korean products enjoy wide access to the U.S. market, and the U.S. is a foreign investor in the growing economic power.

According to the Congressional Research Service, U.S. military aid from 1945 to 2002 to South Korea totaled $8.8 million and economic assistance weighed in at $6 billion. Both forms of aid stopped in the mid-70s.

South Korean development began to make progress when ROK Army Major General Park Chung-hee rode a bloodless coup (called the 5.16 Revolution) to power on May 16, 1961. Park understood Korean rural poverty, having been a countryside teacher before pursuing a military career. As President, he not only launched a vigorous, export-led economic development plan, but, remembering countryside poverty, instituted the Saemaul Plan to socio-economically develop rural communities. So impressive was Park's record of economic development that even his long-time political foe, Kim Dae Jung, who Park tried to have killed, praised Park's contributions to Korea's economic development.

While Park's success at economic development drew the praise of many inside and outside of Korea, his authoritarian, despotic ways continued to grow. The U.S. wished that Park would ease up; however, in the prevailing Cold War environment, he produced stability in a crucial part of Asia, while the U.S. was focusing its attention on Vietnam. In 1972, Park produced the "Yushin" Constitution, which was his tool to extend his stay in the Blue House (official presidential residence) for an indefinite number of six-year terms.

Park felt that it was necessary to provide continuity in leadership to ensure Korea's security and stability. To Park, the strategic character of Asia was changing. The Nixon Doctrine of 1969 declared that Asian countries needed to do more to enhance their own security and could only count on non-combat U.S. assistance. Moreover, in 1972, Nixon reached out to China by visiting Beijing.

From the time of the March First Movement, in 1919, which was led by demonstrating university students and sought the independence of Korea from Japan, Korean university students have maintained a highly respected position in society. Student demonstrations against the Park government grew in scale, frequency, and violence causing Park to become ever more authoritarian and repressive. Consequently, on October 26, 1979, Park was assassinated by Kim Jae-kyu, his director of the Korean CIA, who declared he acted out of a sense of patriotism and because Park had seriously undermined the development of Korean democracy. Some suspected that the U.S. had tired of Park's ways and wanted him out of the way.

Choi Kyu-hah, Prime Minister, assumed the Presidency. In December 1979, Major General Chun Doo-hwan, with the support of Hanahoi, a group of similarly minded junior generals, put Army Chief of Staff, General Chung Sung-hwa under house arrest. In April 1980, Chun coerced the weak Choi into appointing him KCIA director. On May 17, 1980, Chun expanded martial law, abolished the National Assembly, arrested a number of politicians, and sentenced left wing Kim Dae-jung to death against American government wishes. The situation was far beyond Choi's control who resigned in August, and Chun became President.

Nationwide protests erupted! The most uncontrollable protest took place in Gwangju, the then capital of South Jeolla Province, in the southwest corner of Korea, which also happened to be the home base of long-time government critic Kim Dae-jung. Protesting crowds, estimated to exceed 300,000, killed a few policemen with stolen weapons, and burned down a radio station. To quell the protest, soldiers of the Korean Special Warfare

Command were taken off of the demilitarized zone dividing North and South Korea and deployed to Gwangju. To move the troops required the approval of the UN Commander, a U.S. general, who was loathe to make such a decision without approval from Washington.

Fearing that North Korea might capitalize on the confusion by launching an attack, key Carter administration officials, including then Deputy Secretary of State Warren Christopher and then Assistant Secretary of State for East Asian and Pacific Affairs Richard C. Holbrooke, approved the deployment and initial use of force. A second use of force, on May 22, was authorized after securing assurances that the Chun administration would work for long-term political reform. According to official ROK statistics, 207 protesters were killed; however, the BBC reported the number was somewhere between 1,000 and 2,000. In large part because of what became known as the "Gwangju Massacre," which lasted from May 18 to 27, 1980, America's image in South Korea has greatly suffered, especially with those born after the Korean War.

South Koreans perceive that the U.S. acts more favorably towards Japan and U.S. allies, than it does towards Korea. This has been especially true in regard to the Status of Forces Agreement which, in part governs, how U.S. service personnel should be treated by legal authorities in the countries where they are stationed. Koreans see the U.S. as being more willing to allow U.S. service personnel to be sequestered and prosecuted in the legal systems of other countries than through the Korean system, despite amendments that have been made to the agreement to address Korean concerns. Dr. Steven Kim of the Asia Pacific Center for Security Studies feels that the U.S. government and military have become much more effective in addressing Korean sensitivities.

A growing number of Koreans question whether U.S. troops should still be stationed in the country, claiming that Korean troops are more sophisticated, better trained, and better equipped than ever before. Others are wary about the political consequences Korea might face in its burgeoning relationship with China, if U.S. troops in Korea were ever deployed to confront a crisis in the Taiwan Strait. There has long been a feeling that the commander of all troops in Korea, both Korean and foreign, should be a Korean. Many have demanded that U.S. 8th Army Headquarters move out of Yongsan. Not only is the base occupying prime real estate in central Seoul, but it also served as Japanese military headquarters during the colonial era, something that Koreans are always sensitive about.

On February 23, Defense Secretary Robert Gates and Korean Minister of Defense Kim Jang-soo agreed on the transfer of operational control of U.S. troops to a Korean commander in July of this year and wartime control in 2012. The U.S. military will move out of Yongsan, and according to the *Korea Herald* return fifty-nine other facilities between now and 2011.

There is growing optimism that the Six-Party Talks will achieve the denuclearization of North Korea. However, reaching this point has been particularly difficult. China and South Korea both want a denuclearized North Korea but emphatically do not want a regime change in the North for fear of the resulting chaos, economic dislocation, and waves of refugees that would flow south into South Korea and north into China. While the U.S.'s stated position was that it wanted denuclearization, South Korea and China came to believe that the U.S.'s real goal was to bring about a change in government. Starting with the administration of Kim Dae-jung, the ROK has based its approach towards North Korea on Kim's "Sunshine Policy" that seeks to engage the North in dialogue and any other possibly constructive act. Against the wishes of South Korea, the U.S. refused to talk one on one with North Korea until just recently.

Negotiations started in 2006 to work out a KORUSFTA, whose scale is that of the North American Free Trade Agreement and would greatly liberalize trade between the two countries. It also could be a great step forward in improving the overall ROK-U.S. alliance. Writing in the Pacific Forum's *PacNet Newsletter*, Troy Stagarone, Director of Congressional Affairs and Trade for the Korea Economic Institute of America says, "the KORUSFTA can help to move the alliance beyond its historical roots in the conflict with North Korea and begins [sic] to develop a more permanent and sustainable dimension to the alliance." Talking with Yonhap News, Deputy U.S. Trade Representative Karen Bhatia said, "If an [KORUS]FTA is signed between South Korea and the U.S., their alliance will be strengthened." Passage of the FTA depends on the Korean National Assembly and U.S.

Congress supporting it in the face of growing organized labor chagrin in both countries. The new influence of the Democratic Party in the U.S. Congress is also of growing concern.

Recent leaders of both countries have held divergent views. Former President Kim Dae Jung and President Bush disagreed over Kim's Sunshine Policy. Both lame ducks, Presidents Roh Moo-hyun, a liberal, and Bush, a conservative, stand at opposite ends of the political spectrum and do not maintain a close relationship. Both suffer low approval ratings in their respective countries, and both presidents' parties have lost legislative majorities. On December 19, there will be a presidential election in South Korea. At the moment, a leading favorite is Ms. Park Geun-hye, daughter of the late President Park and former head of the Grand National Party, a conservative party that has traditionally held pro-American views. On February 12, she addressed students at Harvard University's Kennedy School of Government underlining the need for better ROK-American relations.

Relations between countries are not static and experience ups and downs. The relationship between the ROK and America—traditionally close friends—has been in free fall far too long. Fortunately, there are growing signs that the relationship will pull its self out of the slump.

Old Friends, Reinvigorated Alliance
Honolulu, December 9, 2007

Maintaining the U.S strategic position in Northeast Asia depends on strengthening and renewing the U.S. relationship with the Republic of Korea (South Korea). Besides enhancing regional stability, Korea offers the U.S. a burgeoning market and growing investment opportunities.

To simply anchor the U.S. position in Northeast Asia on a close relationship with Japan is shortsighted. In *Beyond Bilateralism-US-Japanese Relations in the New Asia-Pacific*, Ellis Krauss and T.J. Pempel have co-edited a cogent argument that the Japanese-American relationship has moved beyond the point where Japan blindly follows the U.S. lead in foreign policy for unhampered access to the U.S. market. Instead, the growing Chinese market has surpassed the U.S. market in importance to Japan and was the key factor in lifting Japan out of long-term recession. Differences over economic burden-sharing of U.S. forces in Japan, military cooperation in Iraq and Afghanistan, and priorities in the Six-Party Talks have raised doubts about a closer strategic relationship evolving. Moreover, new Japanese Prime Minister Fukuda Yasuo is primarily concerned with improving Japan's relationship with Asia and might not lend Japanese support to future U.S. foreign policy ventures.

Since the Guangju Massacre in 1980, there has been a definite distancing in traditionally close U.S.-ROK relations. Former South Korean President Kim Dae-jung and President George W. Bush maintained a poor relationship. Bush was opposed to Kim's conciliatory Sunshine Policy, which sought greater interaction with North Korea and de-emphasized treating Pyongyang as an implacable enemy. Kim's successor and current ROK President Roh Moo-hyun has carried on Kim's Sunshine Policy, which helped to create differences in the U.S.-ROK approach to the Six-Party Talks. Initially, the U.S. sought regime change and refused to talk to North Korea one on one, while South Korea feared the collapse of North Korea and urged the U.S. to talk directly to North Korea. Moreover, younger South Koreans are not as enamored with the U.S. as their parents, and many seek the withdrawal of U.S. forces from Korea. Since the establishment of diplomatic relations with China in 1992, the ROK has often appeared more concerned in developing its relationship with Beijing than with Washington.

Timely opportunities exist to improve U.S.-ROK relations. The December 19th ROK presidential election will likely be won by the Grand National Party candidate, Lee Myung-bak. At the time of writing, Lee had a solid lead in various polls. A GNP presidential victory could help lead to a GNP victory in the 2008 National Assembly elections. Unlike Mr. Kim's or Mr. Roh's parties, the GNP traditionally holds positions closer to those of the U.S.

Passage of the Korea-U.S. Free Trade Agreement (KORUSFTA) by both the U.S. Congress and the Korean

National Assembly offers both strategic and economic advantages to the U.S. "The [KORUS]FTA can become a foothold, a base from which the U.S. will be able to engage directly in the region's economic and security-related activities," according to Dr. Il SaKong, Chairman and CEO, Institute for Global Economics; former ROK Minister of Finance; and member of the East-West Center's Board of Governors.

A free trade Agreement can be a useful strategic tool to promote American policy. The U.S.-Singapore FTA allows the U.S. to radiate its influence through the Association of Southeast Asian Nations, helping to dilute growing Chinese influence. The U.S.-Bahrain FTA serves as an anchor for promoting U.S. influence in the Persian Gulf. According to Mr. Terashima Jitsuro, President of the Mitsui Strategic Research Institute, "Asia will account for 50% of global GDP by 2050." Situated in the center of Northeast Asia and very energetically promoting itself as the hub of a more vibrant, multilaterally focused region, a FTA with Korea offers the U.S. the advantages that Dr. Il suggests. Trade and access to the U.S. market is a proven instrument of U.S. foreign policy. A defeated FTA will hinder U.S. leadership and credibility throughout the region. Rather than limiting China's growing influence, the absence of a KORUSFTA will create a void that China will quickly seek to strategically fill.

The purely economic advantages of an FTA are clear. The Korean economy is the world's tenth largest, and Korea is the U.S.'s seventh largest trading partner. Korea is the sixth largest importer of U.S. agricultural goods. In 2006, two way trade was $78 billion, total Korean investment in the U.S. was $16.7 billion, and the U.S. had $36.6 billion invested in Korea. It is estimated that both nations' economies will grow by $10 billion annually due to greatly reduced duties and tariffs on two way trade.

As a result, U.S. exports of consumer and industrial products could increase by 54% and agricultural exports by 200%, yielding special benefit to grains, produce, citrus, beef, and pork, according to the International Trade Commission. The KORUSFTA will provide greater transparency, and an opportunity to participate in the financial services market, to own telecommunications facilities, and to enhance intellectual property rights and enforcement. A KORUSFTA would likely increase Hawaii exports of tropical fruits, nut products, and rendering of professional services in Korea.

Congressional objection to passage of the KORUSFTA lies in Congressional Democrats' negative view of globalization. Moreover, such pessimism is very strongly reflected by Chrysler and Ford which maintain that a KORUSFTA would not guarantee access to the Korean auto market. While Korea has offered to resolve such U.S. automobile industry concerns by removing the 8% tariff on passenger cars, changing the auto tax system on large engines, and modifying emission and other standards, Chrysler and Ford maintain that non-tariff barriers will remain and seek a guaranteed percentage of the market.

An additional obstacle to passage is beef. Once the third largest importer of U.S. beef, Korea now only allows the import of boneless beef due to lingering concern about the mad cow disease in the U.S. The U.S. seeks complete liberalization of U.S. beef in the Korean market.

With President Roh's influence, the National Assembly is set to pass the KORUSFTA. The principal Korean objection to the KORUSFTA came from Korean farmers who did not welcome international competition. President Roh expended great effort in winning over farmers. Moreover, the Korean government has set up a fund to financially assist farmers who suffer from increased trade.

Congressional passage of the KORUSFTA guarantees the U.S. strategic advantage that China craves; economically, China, Canada, and the European Union are set to pounce if the U.S. does not act now.

Pax Americana-Koreana?
Honolulu, May 11, 2008

My week of meeting with various representatives of the Republic of Korea (ROK) government, scholars, and media types has left me optimistic about improved ROK-U.S. relations.

Korean-American relations have been poor during the last ten years. The United States was unenthusiastic about

President Kim Dae-jung's Sunshine Policy, which sought engagement with North Korea by offering more carrots than sticks. Kim's five year term expired in 2003. The Sunshine Policy was carried on by President Roh Moo-hyun who rode a wave of anti-Americanism into office.

The new government of Lee Myung-bak, who many call "MB" or "bulldozer" for his aggressive CEO style, promises to be the antithesis of both previous governments. Kim and Roh were both highly nationalistic. Both a popular former mayor of Seoul and Hyundai Engineering and Construction CEO who worked in the Middle East, MB is far more internationally focused. He wants to halt the Sunshine Policy, questioning what concrete advantage it has yielded for the ROK. As he sees it, North Korea must stop nuclear experimentation and weapons development in order to continue benefiting from South Korean largesse.

MB wants Korean-American relations to be the foundation of Korean foreign policy and for Korea and the U.S. to upgrade their relationship to a "strategic alliance." Speaking at a recent U.S.-Korea Business Council dinner, he said that an alliance should deepen and broaden cooperation on global and other issues. A strategic alliance commits both nations to play active roles in UN peacekeeping missions, fight the war on terrorism, address climate change, and spread democracy according to U.S. Ambassador to Korea Alexander Vershbow in the *Korea Herald*. He added, "There's great opportunity to expand the scope of the alliance on security issues and on political and economic issues as well."

Does having a strategic alliance mean that Korean and American foreign policies act in tandem regardless of the problem or situation, wherever in the world? In other words, does Lee aspire for a relationship that might be called "Pax Americana-Koreana?" Or does he want a relationship characterized by a high degree of mutual intermeshment of goals with a more regional, Northeast Asia focus where Korea is actively involved in the Six-Party Talks and in promoting regional economic cooperation?

Specific policy questions remain: Would a strategic alliance assure the ROK's participation in the U.S. created Proliferation Security Initiative (PSI), which seeks to halt the proliferation of North Korean nuclear weaponry and technology on the high seas by boarding North Korean vessels suspected of transporting such? The Roh administration was adamantly against the PSI since it contradicted the Sunshine Policy and might militarily provoke Pyongyang to retaliate against Seoul, which is always vulnerable to well protected North Korean artillery.

Another litmus test of a strategic alliance involves the unhampered deployment of American troops in Korea to other parts of Northeast Asia and beyond. Roh was firmly opposed to the use of U.S. Forces Korea in any defense of Taiwan. Now officials and defense experts insist that it is the U.S.'s right to use its troops in whatever manner it sees fit; however, they also agree that we might have to wait until an incident actually happens in the Taiwan

Strait to know how Korea will respond.

From Washington's perspective, Korea's security volte-face is clearly a welcomed change. Yet it should not be forgotten that MB's Grand National Party only holds a razor thin majority of 153 seats in the 299 seat unicameral National Assembly where he is confronted with vociferous domestic critics such as Sohn Hak-kyu, leader of liberal United Democratic Party, who still support the Sunshine Policy. While Lee was visiting the U.S. promoting a security alliance, Kim Dae-jung was in the U.S. defending the Sunshine Policy. And while Lee was promoting a strategic alliance, he as just as vigorously campaigning for passage by the U.S. Congress of the Korean-U.S. Free Trade Agreement that has encountered considerable election year difficulty in the Democratic controlled Congress. Just how a strategic alliance might be affected if the GNP should split, as Korean political parties often do, or the FTA falls victim to U.S. Presidential politics remains to be seen.

Happy that 28,500 U.S. troops will remain in Korea and overlooking no possible way to cajole Congressional passage of the FTA, it might seem that South Korea is exclusively dependent on the U.S. In fact, the traditional bilateral security and economic basis of U.S.-Korean relations is beginning to operate in tandem with a more multilateral security and economic focus.

Geographically situated in the center of Northeast Asia, Korea is surrounded by large, powerful neighbors. China controlled Korea, Japan colonized Korea, and Russia sought to subject Korea. From time to time, there is doubt about America's defense commitment to Korea which has made the ROK seek additional measures to ensure its security. Consequently, the ROK is the most dedicated advocate of multilateral security or a new balance of power system in Northeast Asia that is backed by those countries (South and North Korea, China, Russia, Japan, and the U.S.) that have participated in the Six-Party Talks. In such a system, each nation, not just the U.S., plays a balancing role.

Having become so accustomed to a bilateral approach, it has taken the U.S. some time to accept the multilateral security approach. However, in the *Korean Herald*, former White House top Asian expert, Michael Green reminds readers that all three presidential candidates support the approach, indicating that the new U.S. approach is growing roots. Economically, Korea participates in various organizations such as the Honolulu-based Northeast Asia Economic Forum that advocates multilateral economic cooperation.

Given the brutal nature of Japanese colonialism in Korea from 1910 to 1945, Korean-Japanese relations are often sensitive. The Roh administration's relationship with Japan was poor due to excessive Japanese rightist political activity and statements reminiscent of imperial Japan. Lee's approach is predicated on the notion that the past should not be forgotten, yet it should not dictate the future. It is refreshing to hear a ROK president declare that he wants "a mature relationship with Japan." Furthermore, creating a better relationship with Japan is an important building block in bringing about two other dimensions of Lee's foreign policy: the Seoul-Tokyo-Washington triangle and the Seoul-Tokyo-Beijing triangle. "Seoul will be able to focus its trilateral ties with Washington and Tokyo on hard power or security while, at the same time, fostering another trilateral link with Washington and Beijing—this one centering on economic and soft power," said Jin Chang-soo of the Sejong Institute, a private think tank.

Once the closest of friends with much in common historically, politically, and economically, there is little chance of an improvement in relations between Seoul and Taipei. China is Korea's most important market and plays an important role in multilateral security affairs. Likewise, through promotion of the Seoul-Washington-Beijing triangle, the ROK is signaling its security and foreign policy should not in any way be misconstrued as an attempt to contain China.

To enhance its global image, Korea needs to further promote its growing developmental assistance programs. Beginning with the land reform of 1945-1950 and the Saemaul-New Village Movement of 1971, Korea has gained broad experience in economic development to share with the developing world. These lessons are taught to officials from developing countries at the Korea Development Institute. In other cases, the Korea International Cooperation Agency promotes training in various aspects of development through contracts with universities. At an annual budget of $744 million in 2005, officials acknowledged that Korea's Official Development Assistance (ODA) program is small, and that much of the ODA is "tied," requiring recipient nations to buy Korean goods. Tying aid is a common practice among donor nations. Donor nations also target aid to support strategic and economic goals. Not surprising then is that the bulk of Korean ODA is focused on Northeast Asia and Korea's main source of oil, the Middle East. It remains to be seen how Korea and U.S. developmental assistance might be coordinated in a Korean-American strategic alliance.

ROK-U.S. relations are on a positive upswing. However, the strategic alliance notion needs time to evolve and to let the U.S. become more acquainted with the Lee administration which only took office in February. The ROK would do well to remember there will be a new U.S. President in January 2009.

South Korea and Taiwan: Economic Dragons and Vibrant Democracies
Honolulu, May 13, 2007

Upcoming presidential elections in both South Korea and Taiwan could help to improve the U.S.'s relations with both.

South Korean President Roh Moo-hyun cannot succeed himself.

According to the *Korea Times*, with the support of 60% of the electorate, the Grand National Party (GNP) appears to be on the road to victory in this December's presidential election. The GNP stands for close relations with the U.S., Japan, and the West while taking a hard line on North Korea, positions all contrary to those advocated by President Roh.

Yonhap News reports that leading GNP presidential aspirants Lee Myung-bak, former Seoul mayor and former top Hyundai Group executive, and Park Geun-hye, the daughter of assassinated President Park Chung-hee and a former GNP Chair, are responding to popular demand by focusing on economic growth. With a 40% favorable rating, Lee is promoting his "7.4.7 Vision." In other words, Lee aims to create a 7% growth rate, with a $U.S.40,000 per capita gross national product, building the economy into the seventh largest in the world by 2010. Following with a 20% favorable rating, Park has promoted ideas to bring the Korean stock market index up to the 3,000 point level despite that it only recently passed the 1,500 point.

Things seem to be going well for the GNP; however, there are problems. Squabbling over the party's primary candidate selection process and a stinging defeat in the September 26 by-election amidst allegations that some candidates paid bribes to secure their nominations, rumors pervaded that the party will split in two. Although the dictatorial period in South Korean history, which is largely remembered as the era of Generals and Presidents Park Chung-hee and Chun Doo-hwan, ended with the creation of direct Presidential elections in 1987, the GNP is still often associated with that period.

The ruling Uri Party, one time party of President Roh,

only registers a 10% approval rating among South Korean voters. Thirty-two Uri National Assembly members recently resigned from the party, sacrificing the party's majority in the assembly, and seeking to create another party with a better image. Separately, former Uri Chairs Chung Dong-young and Kim Geun-tae may both bolt the party by the end of May resulting in an additional loss of thirty members. Talk abounded about a possible coalition between former Uri assembly members and other South Korean political parties such as the Democratic Party (DP) and Democratic Labor Party. When no coalition could be negotiated with the DP, twenty former Uri members created a new party, on May 7, that they hoped would grow in strength and ultimately be an attractive coalition partner with other parties. Besides the lack of direction displayed by all opposition entities, the GNP is the only party with viable candidates.

Given the relative unraveling of the U.S.-South Korean Alliance under liberal South Korean governments, a GNP victory in the December 19th presidential election would help to stabilize the relationship.

Setting the stage for the March 8, 2008 presidential elections in Taiwan are the December 2007 parliamentary (legislative yuan) elections.

The upcoming parliamentary elections will represent a change from elections based on multi-member districts to single member districts. The number of seats will be cut from 225 to 133. Those who advocated change not only claimed that parliament had far too many members, but also the members were not well qualified and that parliament was inefficient.

According to Richard Bush, former Chairman and Managing Director of the American Institute in Taiwan, multi-member districts allow an individual party to run several candidates in the same district in order to gain as many of the allotted seats as possible. Therefore, parties tended to become factionalized as candidates staked out rather shrill positions to differentiate themselves from other members in their own party. In such a competitive atmosphere, it has been convenient to advocate anti-Peoples' Republic of China (PRC) positions. Bush concludes that parliament is a chorus of extreme voices.

Like President Roh, President Chen cannot succeed himself. Former Premier and Mayor of Kaohsiung Frank Hsieh (Hsieh Chang-ting) has been selected as the Democratic Progressive Party (DPP) Presidential candidate, besting outgoing President Chen Sui-bian's protégé and Premier Su Tseng-chang by a tally of 44% to 33%. Hsieh wants to improve relations with China and rev up Taiwan's economy. Yet, the DPP has stubbornly promoted Taiwan independence, despite a fall in popular support. Hsieh, a founder of the DPP and an attorney, prominently defended Taiwan independence activists in the wake of the Kaohsiung Incident when Taiwan was under martial law. Moreover, his likely Vice-Presidential running mate is Yeh Chu-lan. According to the *China Post*, Yeh is the widow of Nylon Deng, a martyr who immolated himself in 1989 as a protest for freedom of the press. Yeh is closely identified with independence activists.

Under Hsieh, the DPP might develop a more friendly approach towards China; however, the Kuomingtang (KMT) has consistently been more favorable to developing a long-term accommodation with mainland China. One time "Mr. Clean," the former Taipei mayor and recently resigned Chairman of the KMT, Ma Ying-jeou is the Nationalist presidential candidate. Wang Jin-pyng, President of the Legislative Yuan, is a likely vice-presidential candidate. Hailing from Southern Taiwan, Wang was active in the pro-localization faction of the KMT. The faction advocates the study of Taiwanese history and culture, preferring not to see Taiwan as a mere outgrowth of China.

Until questioned by prosecutors regarding alleged embezzlement in November of 2006, Ma Ying-jeou was considered a foregone winner in the 2008 presidential election. Presently, he seems to be regaining traction, yet his stature has been hurt, which will result in a difficult race against Hsieh. President Chen has pushed Taiwan independence too much for both the good of Taiwan, his party's own aspirations, and Taiwan's relations with the U.S. Many supporters in his first run for President withdrew support in his 2004 run when he won by less than a percentage point. Taiwan is at a difficult economic juncture where it can no longer thrive on cheap labor. Many in Taiwan are more concerned about the island's economic future, arguing that independence would not improve the economic situation. Unless Mr. Hsieh does an about-face on Mr. Chen's position on independence,

U.S. interests are better served by a KMT victory, which would help to maintain the U.S.'s primary goal in East Asia: stability, which would benefit all countries.

Whatever the electoral results, South Korea and Taiwan are maturing democracies that are adding excitement and vibrance to East Asian politics.

South Korea Short on Jobs, Investment
Seoul, October 18, 2009

South Korea looks prosperous: Department stores stock a wide variety of upscale, international brand products; well-dressed business people fill the streets of Seoul; and the skyline is one of gleaming, high-rise office and apartment buildings. But economic challenges here persist and require a new economic development model.

Following the East Asian economic model, with its emphasis on cheap labor to fuel export-led economic growth, South Korea became a wealthy country. However, expensive labor and militant labor unions have forced Korean manufacturing to move to areas where labor is cheap, plentiful, and unorganized. The result is increased unemployment at home. South Korea has to find a new model for continued economic growth and increased employment. Given the high cost of living and a growing number of Koreans living paycheck to paycheck, stimulating domestic demand doesn't seem like it could make up for lost exports and jobs.

What's more, according to the *Korea Herald*, "South Korea has experienced the fastest income polarization among the rich Organization for Economic Cooperation and Development nations over the past decade." Since the 1998 Asian financial crisis, the number of low-income people has increased due to a scarcity of jobs. At the same time, those with more financial assets saw rising stock and real estate prices added onto their regular salaries.

To help address the economic malaise, President Lee Myung-bak has lobbied for passage of the Korea-U.S. Free Trade Agreement. Studies have concluded that this would result in a 6 percent rate of growth in the South Korean gross domesic product over a 10-year period. Although the U.S. economy would grow by $10 billion to $11 billion annually, U.S. resistance has come from the cattle industry, which has encountered barriers in exporting beef to South Korea. And those in the automobile industry fear that a free trade agreement would only add to the imbalance in the automobile trade between the two countries. A compromise is clearly in the economic interests of both countries. ROK ambassador to Washington Han Duck-soo predicts that the U.S. will ultimately pass the agreement early next year, after the health care reform issue is settled.

To keep a manufacturing base and expand job opportunities, South Korea has to develop higher-value-added high-tech products. With greater innovation and added creativity, South Korean manufacturing might be able to move away from the highly disciplined "traditional" manufacturing it has been known for, into the aerospace engineering, bio-engineering, and environmentally-oriented "green" industries.

Another way to invigorate the economy is to improve the foreign investment environment. According to a Korea Chamber of Commerce and Industry survey conducted among five hundred foreign firms, the South Korean investment environment was rated behind that of Singapore, Hong Kong, and Taiwan in terms of incentive programs, deregulation efforts, and legal consistency. Lee clearly understands the situation and is trying to improve the investment environment, but is running into bureaucratic resistance.

As beneficial as the free trade agreement would be to South Korea's economic woes, the solution to its economic challenges is multifaceted.

No Trump: Playing the China Card in North Korea
Honolulu, May 18, 2005

Locked into its own overzealous, simplistic, and dogmatic world view, it's no wonder that the Bush administration's hope to play the China card to contain North Korea's nuclear development has yielded no result.

The U.S. assumed that the denuclearization of North Korea was in both the U.S.'s and China's interest. Clearly, a nuclear free Korean peninsula would enhance America's security interests and protect markets in Northeast Asia.

Even though China doesn't especially want to see North Korea capable of launching nuclear tipped long range missiles, it has little incentive to help the U.S.

As much of a nuisance as its little socialist brother can be, the maintenance of the North Korean regime provides China with a valuable buffer, putting the 32,000 U.S. troops in South Korea 200 miles farther away from China's border. This is especially important to China, since it harbors deep fears that the U.S. is trying to encircle it by building U.S. relations with Central Asian republics such as Afghanistan, Pakistan, India, Vietnam, and Mongolia, not to mention strengthening the U.S. military relationship with Japan and renewing support for Taiwan.

Since the early days of the People's Republic of China, Chinese foreign policy has generally adhered to the Five Principles of Peaceful Co-Existence, which emphasizes mutual non-interference in another country's internal affairs.

China sympathizes with North Korea. China will not take any action that will weaken the North Korean government or make it appear to be party to regime change. North Korea was created with the sacrifice of 500,000 Chinese soldiers who fought American and United Nations troops to a standstill during the Korean War. While China has adapted many free market practices, it was not all that long ago that it found itself in an economic situation similar to North Korea's. China is more open than in the past, but like North Korea, it is still one of a few remaining Communist countries.

Economically, if China were to cut-off food and oil supplies to North Korea, it would only destabilize North Korea and send thousands of refugees to China where the government is already wrestling with large numbers of its own restive, unemployed workers.

Bush administration foreign policy has shunned negotiation and been raucously insistent on achievement of one-sided U.S. policy objectives. At the same time the U.S. is demanding Chinese help in dealing with North Korea, it has done little to satisfy strong Chinese demands to limit U.S. support for Taiwan, continues to call for Chinese currency revaluation, and persists in promoting human rights issues. All of these are clearly important but should take a second seat to American national security and be negotiated in a more constructive bilateral fashion.

Living in Hawaii, the closest state to Korea, our security should be of growing concern. The administration has been playing a bad hand: The China card isn't going to trump North Korea.

Random Views of Asia from the Mid-Pacific

William E. Sharp, Jr.

Chapter Six

JAPAN

The Koizumi Boom
Honolulu, October 23, 2005

Normally, drab, colorless, and non-dynamic, Japanese prime ministers govern on the basis of primus inter pares for two years or less, trying to make as few waves as possible. However, every once in a while a true leader ala Shigeru Yoshida, father of Japan's economic miracle, Tanaka Kakuei, nicknamed the "bulldozer" because of his great ambition and energy, or from 2001, iconoclastic Koizumi Junichiro make their way to the top of Japan's murky political world. Divorced, known for his love of rock music, and his flamboyant mane, Koizumi is uncharacteristically straightforward, not averse to risk taking, and is the take-charge sort of Prime Minister that the U.S. likes to see at the helm of the Japanese ship of state.

His Liberal Democratic Party's (LDP) September 11, 2005 decisive electoral victory gives him control of 296 of 480 seats in the Japanese parliament's lower house, the House of Representatives (HR). Adding the number of seats gained by the LDP's junior coalition partner, the

Buddhist-backed New Komei Party, the coalition has 327 seats in its arsenal. A two-thirds majority is required to override the upper house, the House of Councillors (HC). With such political capital, Koizumi has set a clear path for achievement of his long coveted center piece in Japanese financial reform: the privatization of Japan Post.

Japan's national postal system is far more than just a conveyor for delivering letters and packages. Indeed, it is also a huge bank with deposits of three trillion dollars; privatized, it would be the largest bank in the world. In much the same way that the U.S. Congress uses the Social Security Trust Fund to finance pork barrel "pet" projects, Japanese politicians use Japan Post bank savings accounts to build bridges and highways to nowhere. Koizumi seeks privatization to stem Japan's soaring public debt that stands at 150% of gross domestic product, the highest rate in any industrialized country, and as a way to make more capital available for more efficient market distribution.

Despite Koizumi having brought stability to Japan's banking system, reduced the influence of "zoku" or groups of Diet members that promote a particular industry's interests to the public's detriment, and centralized control over factions, which are groups of LDP Diet members, often led by former prime ministers, that encumber party unity, reaching this point wasn't easy. Achieving his historic electoral victory underlies Koizumi's determination. His previous attempt in August to privatize Japan Post failed to gain enough votes in the HC and given the LDP coalition's pre-election number of seats in the HR, there was no way to have overridden the upper house. Dissolving the HR and calling for a September 11 lower house election, Koizumi vigorously created a victorious strategy.

First, as president of the LDP, he withheld election support to thirty-seven LDP rebels (twenty were not re-elected) who had voted against his first postal privatization bill. To run against them, he recruited "shikaku" (assassins), many of whom are high profile women. Secondly, Koizumi showed a keen ability to use the media to his advantage just as some of Japan's more dynamic prime ministers had; for example, Nobel Prize winner Sato Eisaku, Tanaka Kakuei, and Nakasone Yasuhiro.

A record breaking 67.5 percent of eligible Japanese voters went to the polls. In the post-election special Diet session convened on September 26, the new HR passed postal privatization by a vote of 338 to 138 on October 11, 2005. The HC did likewise by a vote of 134 to 100 on October 14, 2005. Now a law, privatization of the system of 260,000 employees and 25,000 post offices will start in 2007 and conclude in 2017.

As strong and determined as a reformer the Prime Minister is, he has not made any attempt to reduce the influence of the almighty Japanese bureaucracy. Operating in the non-transparent world of Japanese politics, the central government bureaucrats wield great influence over Japanese legislation and are not held accountable to the public. Many see the bureaucracy as inhibiting fiscal reform by maintaining current regulations and disbursements. Staffed with many of Japan's brightest and seen as an important institution that played a central role in Japan's post-war economic miracle, many reformers now call for the role of the bureaucracy to be redefined.

Others protest that while Koizumi has never taken his eye off of postal reform, he has paid precious little attention to national pension and health services reform. Both services are seen by many as more important given Japan's fast aging population. No longer the economic power of the 1980s, Japan cannot raise additional revenue by increasing income taxes or by using the controversial consumption tax. Doing so would retard Japanese economic activity, which is just now showing signs of stable growth. Thus, Japan must more rationally manage its assets. Economically, the U.S. benefits from a more robust Japan that is better equipped to stimulate global economic growth and stability.

The Japanese-American defense relationship is closer than it has ever been, and the relationship between Koizumi and Bush verges on the "Ron-Yasu" relationship effected by President Ronald Reagan and Prime Minister Nakasone Yasuhiro. The Japanese Self-Defense Force has become more internationally visible and is supporting the U.S. in Iraq. In November, to celebrate the 50th anniversary of the LDP, the Prime Minister wants to announce the draft of a new constitution, which will offer an amendment to Article 9, making it easier for the Japanese military to play a more significant international role. A more active defense role has long been advocated by the U.S. While Japan has become more and more dependent on the Chinese market to re-inflate its economy, the Sino-Japanese political relationship is at its lowest point since 1972 when the two countries reestablished diplomatic relations. Relations with North and South Korea are similarly poor. A major cause of such poor relations with its Asian neighbors is Koizumi's repeated visits to Yasukuni Shrine. The shrine glorifies Japan's military past and enshrines fourteen Class-A war criminals who sought destruction of Korea's cultural identity and directed the Imperial Japanese army to burn, kill, or destroy wherever it went in China during World War II.

During his recent election campaign, Koizumi repeatedly said that he would step down as LDP President when his term is up in late 2006. Will he? Former Prime Minister Nakasone was able to extend his tenure after privatizing the Japan National Railway System in the 1980s. Having privatized Japan Post, Koizumi can now go after the Public Highway Corporation, another pork incubator.

A Hard Act to Follow: Who Will Succeed PM Koizumi?
Honolulu, July 9, 2006

Japan's most effective prime minister (PM) since Tanaka Kakuei (1972-1974), the flamboyant, unconventional, Elvis Presley mimicking Koizumi

Junichiro will step down as PM in September. During his five year tenure, he exerted greater control over his Liberal Democratic Party's (LDP) feuding "habatsu" or factions, stabilized Japan's financial system, privatized Japan's postal system thus creating the world's largest bank with deposits of $3 trillion, and won endless praise from the U.S. government by bringing about a more internationally active role for Japan's Self-Defense Forces which sent six hundred troops to Iraq. His relationship with President Bush rivals that of Bush's relationship with British PM Tony Blair.

No one is perfect and neither is Koizumi. While he reinvigorated the Japanese economy by instituting tax cuts for the very wealthy, deregulating, and limiting public works expenditures, the Japanese middle class is contracting. Once known as the society where everyone thought of themselves as "middle class," social cleavage is beginning to appear as is the appellation, "a society of haves and have nots." The world's second wealthiest country continues to experience record setting budget deficits-similar to the world's wealthiest nation, the U.S. Due to his unyielding stance on visiting Yasukuni Shrine, where fourteen World War II Class A war criminals are memorialized, Japan's relations with China and South Korea are frozen in acrimony.

The Japanese PM is not directly elected by Japanese voters. Instead, the PM is elected by members of the majority party in the Diet (parliament), where there are 404 LDP members. The LDP members are not necessarily of one mind due to the role of the factions in

Japanese parliamentary politics. Given the often overwhelming presence of the LDP in the Diet, members organize into factions to more effectively advance or block legislation, to secure campaign funds, and to give them a greater chance of securing a ministerial position. Factions are often led by former PMs. Due to 1996 changes in Japanese electoral law creating single member districts in place of multi-member districts and the stern leadership PM Koizumi exercised over the entire LDP, factions don't have their former influence. Nevertheless, factions influence members' votes for PM and are a critical factor in election strategy. In addition, selection of the PM is dependent on the votes of three hundred local party support groups. The candidate with a majority of votes moves into the PM's residence. Koizumi hasn't expressed any particular support for a successor although many observers feel he supports Abe Shinzo. Overt support might be a plus, but given that many have tired of his strong-willed leadership, it could just as well be a negative.

According to Watanabe Tsuneo of the Mitsui Global Strategic Studies Institute, speculation on Koizumi's successor focuses on four long time politicians: Abe Shinzo, Fukuda Yasuo, Aso Taro, and Tanigaki Sadakazu. At the moment, 52 year old Chief Cabinet Secretary (CCS), Abe Shinzo is the favorite. The CCS position is an extremely important one in Japanese politics and might be likened to the White House Chief of Staff. In Japan's case, many of those who have served in the position went on to become PM. Abe is also a former foreign minister whose father, Abe Shintaro, served in the same position and nearly made it to the PM's Office. His grandfather was Kishi Nobusuke a former PM and suspected World War II war criminal who was very friendly to the U.S. Like his grandfather, Abe is very conservative, deeply contemptuous of Communists, strongly pro-Taiwan, and believes his duty is to protect Japanese people. Some believe Abe has been too uncompromisingly supportive of Koizumi's visits to Yasukuni Shrine. Abe is a member of the large Mori faction. A June 27th poll conducted by the *Asahi Shimbun* tallied 45% of respondents preferring Abe.

A former CCS, who resigned in May 2005 admitting that he was not making payments to the national pension plan, 69-year-old Fukuda Yasuo is the second most favorite to succeed Koizumi. Also politically conservative, Fukuda is the son of former Japanese PM Fukuda Takeo. Before entering electoral politics in 1990, he worked as a section chief at Maruzen Oil Company, as a political secretary to his father, and as a director of the Kinzai Institute for Financial Affairs. Fukuda is a strong supporter of "Nichibei kankei" (Japanese-American relations); however, like his father, his greatest attribute might very well be his concern for improving Japan's flagging relationship with Asia.

Fukuda Takeo is remembered for the "Fukuda Doctrine," which sought to clarify Japan's Asian policy by recommitting Japan to non-militarism, building a close relationship with the Association of Southeast Asian Nations (ASEAN), and serving as a bridge between

ASEAN and Indochina. Fukuda is a foreign policy realist who understands that poor relations with China are hurting Japan. Since Japan's economic recovery drew a good deal of momentum from the robust Chinese market, Fukuda is a favorite of the Japanese business community while Abe remains more popular with the Japanese man on the street. Speculation is rife about a "New Fukuda Doctrine" that would serve as a bridge between the original Fukuda Doctrine and a future East Asian community. Fukuda is also a member of the Mori faction, which Koizumi also belonged to. Fukuda has objected to the PM's visits to Yasukuni Shrine. *Asahi Shimbun* polling results pegged Fukuda's support at 25%.

Aso Taro, 65, currently serves as Japan's foreign minister. Other ministerial portfolios that he has held include economic and fiscal planning plus internal affairs and communication. Outside of politics, he was President and CEO of Aso Mining, a family business. Like his rivals, Aso's family has a deep history in Japanese politics. His grandfather, Yoshida Shigeru, is arguably Japan's best known and most revered post-war PM, who is largely credited for the nation's economic recovery and subsequent economic growth. Moreover, Yoshida minimized the role of Japan's military and incubated Japan's security dependence on the U.S. Aso is strongly anti-Communist and strongly pro-Washington. Unswervingly supportive of his boss's visits to Yasukuni Shrine, Aso is not well regarded in Asian countries. In fact, his tenure as foreign minister has seen relations with both China and Korea go into deep freeze. He is ever skeptical of China's military build up and once stated that during Japan's colonial rule in Korea that Koreans wanted Japanese names. In reality, it was Japanese policy to have Koreans adopt Japanese names. Aso is a member of the small Kono faction. The June 27th poll registered 5% support for Aso.

Minister of Finance, Tanigaki Sadakazu, 61, previously was Minister of Science and Technology, Minister of Reconstruction, and Minister of Industrial Revitalization. He also has worked as a lawyer. Unlike the others, no family member of his became a political household name. Nevertheless, Tanigaki inherited his Diet seat from his father who also served as a minister of education.

Historically, a high percentage of Japan's politicians and bureaucrats are Faculty of Law, University of Tokyo graduates; however, Tanigaki is the only one in this group of candidates. Perhaps that helps to explain why he is considered the most intellectual and best liked by omnipotent bureaucrats. Yet, his popularity among the general public is low since he believes that Japan's highly unpopular consumption tax must be increased in order to further secure Japan's economic recovery. Some observers comment that Tanigaki's advocacy of an increased consumption tax is indicative of bureaucrats' influence on him at a time when Japanese politics seems to be less molded by government officials. Considered the most pro-China candidate, Japan's right wing, a pillar of the LDP, feels he is likely to be too soft on China. Tanigaki leads his own small faction of 15. With 3%

support in the *Asahi Shimbun* poll, Tanigaki has the largest margin to make up.

With his impressive showing in the *Asahi Shimbun* poll, it might seem that Abe will be the victor; however, as factions begin to jockey for position, interesting possibilities appear as the candidates try to negotiate cross factional support. Former PM Yoshihiro Mori and leader of the large Mori faction could be the biggest loser if he supports Abe and Fukuda, then bolts the faction with his supporters. Mori's faction could then disappear entirely. It's no wonder that Mori is encouraging both candidates to talk with each other.

Whoever wins will be up against a wall of problems. Mitsuru Mizuno, retired Japan Development Bank executive who is currently a professor in the graduate business program at Nihon University, says those problems include keeping up the economic recovery, increasing employment opportunities, shoring up the medical insurance and national pension system, and improving Japan's relations with China and South Korea. Others would add addressing Japan's ever widening income gap and the unpopularity of increasing the consumption tax.

China and Japan: Good Economics, Bad Politics
Honolulu, April 9, 2006

Sino-Japanese relations have fallen to their most

politically acrimonious level since the Asian giants normalized diplomatic relations in 1972. Political relations have become so thorny that Chinese President Hu Jintao and Japanese Prime Minister Koizumi Junichiro do not talk, even when they are attending the same international conference where they assiduously avoid each other. Given the tension enveloping the relationship, it is hard to believe that the late Deng Xiaoping, the father of China's post-1978 economic development and opening up to the world, once said, "China's most important bilateral relationship is with Japan." If there is a silver lining in this troubled relationship, it is the economic complementariness that the countries share and the resulting mutual benefit and regional stability that it can yield in the fastest growing economic area of the world.

Chinese culture, filtered through Korea, provided Japan with much of its basic culture from 600 to 857. After all, Buddhism came from China, as did the Chinese characters used in Japanese. Chinese Confucianism's emphasis on age colors contemporary Japan's social organization and structure. The Chinese emphasis on education is also shared by the Japanese. Both countries are "rice cultures," meaning that the discipline and hard work traditionally associated with rice cultivation is contemporarily reflected in the highly disciplined, hard working characteristics of both the Chinese and Japanese.

Japan held China in high esteem until the advent of Western contact in the mid-1800s. Weak China was unable to defend itself against intruding foreigners, backed by the finest militaries of the day. Japan's view of China began to change from a traditionally Confucian one where Japan looked upon China as a father or elder brother figure that it should respect and subordinate itself to. Fearful that it might share China's fate, Japan began to replace Chinese learning with Western learning.

Over the last 120 years, eight events have played a major role in molding China's nationalistic feelings towards Japan: 1) In 1895, Japan quickly defeated China in Korea in the Sino-Japanese War Victory giving Japan control over Korea, where China long exercised suzerainty, plus Taiwan and Port Arthur (Dalian), a major strategic port in Manchuria (Northeast China); 2) Japan's victory in the Russo-Japanese War of 1904-1905 gave the rising East Asian power control over large parts of Manchuria; 3) In 1915, Japan delivered the "Twenty One Demands" to the Republic of China government. Japan wanted more political and economic control, or China would face military reprisals. Moreover, China would have to buy large quantities of Japanese goods and meet Japanese territorial demands; 4) The Chinese delegation to the Versailles Peace Talks, ending World War I, walked out of the negotiations when it refused to sign documents that would give Japan a sphere of influence in Shandong Province; 5) When word of the Versailles negotiations got back to China, it set in motion one of history's greatest demonstrations and subsequent intellectual revolutions, the May Fourth Movement; 6) In 1931, Japan launched a military conquest for full control of Manchuria, eyeing the region's natural resources and growing market prospects); 7) Six years later, Japan created "Manchukoku," a so called independent Manchuria with Henry Pu Yi as puppet emperor; and 8) Japan set out to swallow all of China in 1937. The Chinese call Japan's tactics to subjugate China "sanguang zhengce" or the "burn all, kill all, loot all" tactic. An estimated ten million Chinese were killed by the Japanese.

After the establishment of the People's Republic of China (PRC) in 1949, there was no diplomatic relationship between China and Japan. Instead, Japan recognized the Republic of China (ROC) on Taiwan as the legitimate government of all of China, owing to American pressure. Then again, the Japanese appreciated ROC president Chiang Kai-shek's speedily repatriating Japanese POWs and waiving payment of any war reparations. Nevertheless, China and Japan re-established their active pre-war commercial relations, now carried out by China-based subsidiaries, with no discernible connection to the major Japanese corporations they actually represented. To operate Japanese built factories and steel mills in China, China needed Japanese spare parts and technical advice; Japan needed the Chinese market.

Announcement of Nixon's February 1972 trip to Beijing, secretly organized by National Security Advisor Henry Kissinger, came as a complete surprise to Japan who had been purposely kept in the dark. One possible explanation holds that China demanded Japan not know until the latest possible moment on the assumption that suspicion and mistrust would be introduced into the

Japanese-American relationship creating a wedge between the two countries. If so, no permanent damage ensued, and Japan quickly proceeded to recognize the PRC, which the U.S. had long persuaded it not to do.

Both countries have benefited from the relationship. China has received $30 billion in Japanese Official Development Assistance and another $31.5 in Japanese foreign direct investment. Not as free with transferring technology as the U.S. and Europe, China has still been the beneficiary of Japanese technical transfer and expertise. Over 150,000 Chinese students are studying at Japanese universities; 64,757 Chinese students are studying at U.S. universities. With an unemployment rate of nearly 30%, China needs the one million jobs that Japanese investment provides. Japan has been able to build new markets and take advantage of cheap Chinese labor.

Chinese show little appreciation of Japanese assistance. Despite seventeen apologies being made by Japan for its barbarous World War II invasion of China and the resulting deaths and destruction, the PRC and individual Chinese consider the apologies insincere. The ultra right wing of the Japanese political spectrum makes every attempt to obscure the savagery of the notorious Nanjing Massacre, claiming that 300,000 deaths is a highly inflated number. The biological experiments conducted on Chinese POWs in Manchuria didn't exist. And it was not a Japanese invasion of China, simply an "advance."

Particularly galling to China are the visits of Japanese

Prime Ministers to Yasukuni Shrine. Yasukuni Shrine honors those who died militarily serving Japan and in some ways is similar to Arlington National Cemetery. However, Yasukuni honors fourteen executed Class A war criminals responsible for ravaging China, including war time Prime Minister Tojo Hideki. Within the grounds of Yasukuni Shrine is the Yushukan, a museum devoted to a very self-righteous view of Japanese military history. Suggestions across the Japanese political spectrum plus Chinese and Korean demands to create a separate memorial for the Class A war criminals have been unsuccessful. Liberal Democratic Party Japanese prime ministers must politically pay homage at Yasukuni in order to appease survivors of the war dead, veterans groups, and the rightist elements of their party. To temporize their visits, prime ministers disingenuously visit as "private citizens." Failure of the Japanese government to prohibit schools' use of history textbooks whitewashing Japan's World War II atrocities is another constant contributing to the bad politics between the two countries.

Owing to corruption, authoritarianism, gaps in wealth between those who have become rich early and those who haven't, as well as the gaps in prosperity between those living in a handful of coastal cities and those living inland, the Chinese Communist Party does not enjoy the support that it once did. To build popular support, it periodically fuels the flames of nationalism by inciting demonstrations and then standing by doing nothing to stop them. Japan is a convenient target for such smoldering nationalism. China's development of the online computer game, "Japan in China 1937-1945," seeks to mold younger public opinion against Japan. "March of the Volunteers," China's snappy national anthem, was created during World War II to stimulate soldiers' patriotism and motivation to fight Japan. As such, it serves up a subliminally anti-Japanese message as some of the lyrics suggest, "Arise, we do not want to be an enslaved people...the Chinese people are at a particularly perilous juncture...facing the enemy's artillery, attack, attack, attack."

As China gains more economic and military power, it sees itself in its traditional role as the "Central Kingdom" where all surrounding nations paid homage to the Emperor of China in Beijing. Ever fearful of American containment by building close relations with bordering nations, China is further motivated to achieve undisputed leadership in Northeast Asia, Southeast Asia, and Central Asia. However, Japan plays an important and largely economic role in those corners of the continent; thus China knows it's unrealistic to expect that Japan will play a subordinate role. It is, moreover, quite clear to China that Japan gains great economic and military strength through its relationship with the U.S. Under the leadership of Prime Minister Koizumi, Japan has been steadily moving away from its post-World War II pacifism, seeking more military clout, and greater influence in international affairs. Japan's bid for a permanent seat with veto power on the UN Security Council threatens China's quest for regional ascendancy since China would not be able to argue that it alone represents Asian interests in the council. Faced with the possibility of Japan's presence on the council, Chinese editorial commentary has become particularly virulent. The February 2 issue of the online *People's Daily* cries out that Japan "chinmeishuya," sucks up to America while it ignores Asia. Despite Chinese propaganda, Japan has greatly benefited economic development throughout Asia.

Strong support of Taiwan by Koizumi cabinet members only further hinders better relations with China. Chinese attempts to isolate Taiwan within Asia have helped to push Taiwan and Japan closer together. As a result, Japan has expressed concern for Taiwan's security, underlining its importance to Japan's security. In addition, the long simmering territorial issue concerning the sovereignty of Diaoyutai (Chinese) or Senkakushoto (Japanese), situated between the southern most tip of Okinawa Prefecture and the northeast coast of Taiwan, seems to have no solution in sight. Both countries' high demand for energy has sparked territorial claims over Chunxiao (Chinese) or Shirakaba (Japanese), a small East China Sea island, rich in natural gas.

Both China and Japan need a stable relationship to underwrite the stability of Asia. Just as both nations need a good relationship to continue on their own paths to economic growth, the economic complementariness that they share should not be lost amid the animosity of anti-Japanese demonstrations and certain policies of Mr. Koizumi, who will leave office in September of this year.

Suggestion that relations could be righted through a regional security organization involving Japan, China, the Koreas, Russia, and the U.S. lack persuasiveness given the failure of those nations to control North Korean nuclear proliferation. Having all of the right ingredients, good economics can make better politics.

Random Views of Asia from the Mid-Pacific

William E. Sharp, Jr.

Chapter Seven

INDIA

India and America: It's the Economy, Stupid!
Honolulu, July 11, 2006

The U.S. should approach its reinvigorated relationship with India as more of a long-term economic relationship than a geopolitical chess move against China.

U.S. relations with independent India have never been quite what one would have hoped. To the dismay of the U.S., Nehru lead, independent India became a key leader of the non-aligned nations movement, which sought a middle ground between the U.S. and then Soviet Union. The U.S. became an ardent supporter of arch enemy Pakistan with whom India fought wars in 1947, 1965, 1971, and 1999. One might have thought that India's defeat in its 1962 war with China could have pushed India closer to the U.S. Instead, India signed a twenty year treaty of friendship with the Soviet Union in 1971 due to its fear of China. As further insurance, India began development of nuclear weapons in 1974 and conducted five underground tests in 1998 (after other powers ceased). Economically, Indian government policies were highly suspicious of foreign investment, reflecting the country's colonial past. Faced with unending regulation, U.S. and other foreign investors invested elsewhere.

For the last twenty-five years, India has had the second fastest growing economy in the world, behind only China. Serving first as the Governor of the Reserve Bank of India in the early 1980s and finance minister in the 1990s, Prime Minister Manmohan Singh is often called the architect of India's economic reform and opening to the world. Since becoming prime minister in 2004, Singh has eliminated the capital gains tax, reduced corporate tax rates, and sought to increase India's economic growth rate to between 7% and 8%. To do so, agricultural growth must continue despite India's ruinous monsoons and poor infrastructure. Foreign direct investment (FDI) has averaged only $5 to $6 billion a year as compared to the $60 in FDI that pours into China annually. India hopes to increase FDI to $10 billion this year.

As a FDI destination, India offers many advantages that China doesn't. Like America, India embraces democracy. Approximately 20% of Indians speak English as a native language. Key Indian service industries have grown at over 9% year after year due to increases in productivity and the incorporation of new technology. The Mumbai-Sensex Index gained 42% for 2005. Stock exchanges and the securities business in India are considered well managed and above board, quite to the contrary of the Shanghai and Shenzhen exchanges in China. The Indian banking industry shares a similar reputation. Conversely, China has a beleaguered banking sector, which is the victim of a high percentage of loans that it will never be able to fully recover and that were made on the basis of political concerns and connections. India has a functioning, codified judicial system; China doesn't. Although 300 million of 1 billion Indians live in poverty, it boasts a middle class of 250 to 300 million and is experiencing a tsunami of consumerism, second only to China's. One-half of all Indians are under twenty-five years of age; China is an aging society. If India had not experienced the growth that it has, Bush would likely not have visited earlier this year.

Based on Dan Fineman's "Growth Model" in the April 15, 2004 edition of the *Far Eastern Economic Review*, India has created its own model of economic development that is distinctly different from the East Asian model. Unlike the East Asian model, the Indian model is not based on a central government developed and monitored industrial policy, which dishes out preferential tax breaks, politically directs lending, and ponies up subsidies. The East Asian Model creates growth, but stock market profits lag behind gross domestic product. Promoting privatization and deregulation, the Indian model reaps higher stock market profits. The Indian model requires less saving, which allows for greater growth of domestic demand. Being more consumption driven, there is less need for export growth. Perpetual trade surpluses can cause economic friction and political problems with trading partners who suffer perennial trade deficits. For example, the U.S.'s deficits with China and Japan. India's model is more sustainable because it rewards the consumer and minimizes trade friction with other countries.

At first glance, India seems to share a good deal with the U.S. English is the communicative adhesive that helps to hold both culturally diverse countries together and connect them to the world. India and America share a strong democratic tradition and share similar economic interests; however, both countries still need time to become better friends. And Americans shouldn't assume that because there are these common points that India sees the world through the neo-conservative blinders that Washington does.

In area and population, India is a huge country with an abundance of human talent. It has a large military, and is one of the world's oldest civilizations, having withstood over three hundred years of British intrusion. Not surprisingly, it is sensitive to foreign bullying. In a recent survey conducted by *Outlook Magazine,* a leading Indian publication, 72% of Indians consider America an international bully and dislike its unilateralist approach to foreign policy. While it talks about halting nuclear proliferation, it is the only leading nuclear power that has actually used nuclear weapons. It talks about the need to control chemical weapons but used them in Vietnam. Interestingly, two-thirds thought that Bush was a friend of India, yet 59% feel that India has compromised its foreign policy goals to create a better relationship with the U.S.

Despite its huge Islamic population of 150 million, India is free of Islamist terror. Javed Akhtar, leader of

Muslims for a Secular Democracy and leading Indian filmmaker, said, "the problem of the world is not Islamic fundamentalism. It is American fundamentalism and American greed for power." Conversely, there are those Indians who would like to see a stronger response to Islamic terror, especially in Kashmir and along India's border with Bangladesh.

The U.S. and India both have legitimate concern over regrowing Chinese military power. They closely watch steady increases in China's military budget and its continued acquisition or development of increasingly sophisticated military weaponry. Many in the U.S. Department of Defense (DOD) warn about China's rise in such publications as the *Quadrennial Defense Report*. Secretary Rumsfeld's strident, blustery tirades are legendary. Some theorize that a strong relationship with Japan in East Asia should be complemented by a strong relationship with India in South Asia. These types of security relationships would force China to divide its attention and resources between two distant locations and limit its ability to spread its influence. Moreover, such geopolitics trigger a key Chinese concern and fear: "containment." Many Chinese leaders and analysts assume that the U.S. wishes to surround China on its borders to prevent it from achieving super power status, just as the U.S. did to the Soviet Union. U.S. officialdom claims that both the U.S. and India do not view China as an enemy.

Chinese diplomacy towards India has been highly active and successful. Within the last year, progress has been made on two long standing border issues with India. Nevertheless, India is concerned by the posting of Chinese naval advisers along the Myanmar coast, soldiers on the Yangon controlled Coco Islands, and growing ties with Bangladesh. Chinese assistance in building a Pakistani submarine base in Gawdar draws close attention. While China seems intent on protecting water routes to Middle East oil, the projection of Chinese naval power into India's maritime and regional zones of interest has brought about a corresponding Indian naval build up. Some wonder if the question shouldn't be the other way around: Does China wish to contain India?

It would seem that both India and America would want to counter growing Chinese influence. However, the Indians, given their colonial experience and size, wish to maintain strategic independence. Put in the words of Robert Blackwell, U.S. Ambassador to India from 2001 to 2003, "there is no better way to empty a drawing room in New Delhi of Indian strategists than to start talking about the idea." India wants to develop its own relationship with China, based on shared interests and to compete for the economic leadership of Asia. While U.S. President Bush's administration proclaimed its wish "to help India become a major world power in the 21st Century," it opposed the building of a gas pipeline from Iran across Pakistan and into India due to deteriorating ties with Iran. America has not supported India's burning wish for a permanent seat on the UN Security Council. During Wen Jiabao's May 2005 visit to India, he expressed China's support for India to join the body, although nothing more was said about it once he had returned to Beijing. Furthermore, China and India engaged in joint naval exercises off of Shanghai in 2003, and India maintains observer status in the Chinese dominated Shanghai Cooperation Organization, which seeks to limit U.S. influence in Central Asia.

In consideration of its relationship with China, India has shown less support for maintaining a refuge for the Dalai Lama. Consequently, his organization has considered moving to the U.S. While a better relationship with America is one strategic option for India, others have appeared. In the early 1990s, the Russians were promoting a triangular relationship combining Russia, China, and India. An April 2004 edition of the *People's Daily* (online) advocated Asia's three giants: China, India, and Japan, form an alliance. The suggestion had a distinct "Asian for Asians" tone and obviously sought to minimize U.S. influence, promising regional stability and economic well being.

At first glance, President Bush's offer to open U.S. civilian nuclear technology to India ostensibly to alleviate demand for natural resources in the international energy market appears to be clever diplomacy. Closer scrutiny reveals a number of problems. India did not sign the Nuclear Non-Proliferation Act. By offering India U.S. nuclear technology, the U.S. signals ipso facto acceptance of India's nuclear program. Although India's nuclear sites are to be divided into military and civilian use facilities, only the civilian use facilities will be open to international inspection by the International Atomic

Energy Association. India will determine the designation of each site, but it is assumed that one-third of the sites will be off limits to inspectors. Too many remember India's broken promise in 1974 that its nuclear development was only for peaceful purposes. Instead, India developed nuclear weapons. There is no guarantee that this arrangement will receive U.S. Congressional approval despite the growing number of lobbying groups. In India, many object to foreign inspection of any kind and feel that the U.S. wants to limit the nuclear weapons program.

The U.S. promotes itself as a country based on law, yet the proposal breaks U.S. and international law. Presenting such a glaring contradiction and double standard to the world only reinforces negative images of the U.S. at a time when its global popularity continues to plunge, suffering from charges of being unilateralist, self-serving, and dogmatic. If the U.S. can help India, can we realistically expect Iran to halt nuclear development? Why should North Korea seriously consider scrapping its nuclear development when the U.S. is helping India's efforts? What will Pakistan ultimately want? Can we afford to alienate Pakistan, a nation that has worked closely with the U.S. in fighting terrorism? How would the political future of President Musharraf, who has survived two assassination attempts for his cooperation with America, be affected?

To try to play the "Indian card" against China will only further prolong development of a relationship that has been too long in coming. The best way to promote a long-term relationship with India is to build on the economic relationship and encourage more investment in India, and less in China. The geopolitics will follow at the right time.

China and India: Dance of the Emerging Giants
Honolulu, July 13, 2008

In 2005, Chinese diplomacy promised great flexibility and suggestions of compromise in resolving long standing border issues with India. During his 2005 trip to New Delhi, Premier Wen Jiabao talked of sponsoring a permanent seat for India on the United Nations Security Council. Fast forwarding to 2008, China's position on the border issues shows no flexibility, and there is no meaningful discussion of supporting an Indian seat on the council.

The border issues revolve around the 56,000 square mile Arunchal Pradesh, an Indian state the size of Portugal in Northeast India bordering China's Tibet Autonomous Region, and Aksai Chin, a 16,000 square mile area bordered by India's northern most state, Jammu, and Kashmir, and both China's Tibet and Xinjiang Autonomous Regions. Arunchal Pradesh is currently controlled by India but claimed by China; Aksai Chin is controlled by China and claimed by India.

China's view is that India's claim to Arunchal Pradesh is invalid. The Chinese say that the McMahon Line separating Tibet from India was the product of the 1914 Simla Convention conducted by Britain and Tibet and that Tibet did not have the power to negotiate a treaty in that it didn't have sovereignty. Moreover, no Chinese government or any sovereign government recognized Tibet's 1913 declaration of independence. In 1915, the British stated that neither China nor Russia accepted the Simla Convention and it was therefore invalid.

Chinese People's Liberation Army (PLA) incursions across the border into Arunchal Pradesh are more and more frequently reported. Consequently, it has become clear to New Delhi that this remote part of India is ill defended and is further vulnerable due to poor roads and no rail or air service connecting it to the rest of India. The lack of infrastructure and connectivity is a major barrier in rapidly deploying Indian troops to the area in event of an emergency. On the Chinese side, the roads, availability of electricity, and other facilities are much better.

Achieving no progress on border issues during a state visit to Beijing from January 2008, Prime Minister Manmohan Singh set about upgrading infrastructure in Arunchal Pradesh and creating educational and health care facilities.

Aksai Chin adjoins the Ladakh District of Jammu and Kashmir State. It is part of the Tibetan Plateau, largely uninhabited, has no permanent settlements, and has little rainfall. In the early 1950s, China encroached on Aksai Chin to build a strategically important road connecting Tibet and Xinjiang. India has recently reopened an old air force base in Ladakh.

Although it recognized Sikkim as an integral part of India in 2003 and changed its maps to reflect such, PLA troops have made recent incursions into the mountainous Indian state.

Such Chinese incursions and stiffening of territorial demands over the last two years are seen by many as an attempt to put pressure on India to bolster Beijing's claim to disputed areas, according to the *Times of India*.

Undoubtedly, the purely territorial motivation has validity. However, there are other causative factors explaining China's about face.

India is a rising regional and global economic and political competitor.

India's "Look East" policy, which seeks to cultivate economic and security relations with Southeast Asian nations, strikes at what China normally sees as its strategic underbelly and a region where it has traditionally had great influence. China has actively courted the Association of Southeast Asian Nations (ASEAN) and opposed the inclusion of India in ASEAN Plus Three (China, Korea, and Japan). The Chinese showed no interest in India's ideas about creating a regional security apparatus as outlined by Indian Foreign Minister Pranab Mukherjee in his June speech at Beijing University.

India recognizes China's claim to Tibet; however, it hosts the Dalai Lama led Tibetan government in exile and 100,000 Tibetan refuges. Given the harsh measures employed by Chinese security personnel in quelling the recent Tibetan riots, China is clearly worried about the possibility of Tibet spinning out of its control. Tibet on one hand is a kind of buffer zone between China proper and India, while on the other hand the Chinese are worried about a chain reaction. A Tibet that slipped out of China's grasp could well cause the Xinjiang Autonomous Region to declare independence.

China is concerned about India's chumming up with the U.S. Of particular concern is growing security and economic cooperation, plus possible transfer of U.S. civilian nuclear energy technology. It is clear that the U.S. is joined by Japan and Australia in seeing India as a potential security and economic counterweight to China. China is perpetually worried about being surrounded by unfriendly nations and alliances, especially if the U.S. is involved. As a result, it sees cooperation such as the 2007 Malabar naval exercises joined by the U.S., Japan, and Australia as an attempt to encircle it.

If Chinese fears have substance, then the Indians have an equal right to be concerned about being surrounded by China. After all, Tibet borders India. China has naval advisors in mainland Myanmar (Burma), intelligence gathering facilities on Great Coco Island in the Bay of Bengal, and is planning to build an army base on Little Coco Island. China built a port in Bangladesh and in Sri Lanka. There is fear that the Chinese navy might use the ports, just as there is worry that China might use the Pakistani naval facilities at the port of Gawdar, Pakistan, that it is helping to build. The Chinese claim that the ports are for strictly commercial purpose; yet it is clear that China wants to have the means to protect the sea lanes to ensure unimpeded transport of crude oil from the Middle East to China. To the Indians, China's posture in South Asia and on the Indian Ocean represents an intrusion into an area where Indian influence has gone unchallenged. India's naval build up hopes to add one carrier this year and another in 2011, as well as build its submarine fleet to control the Indian Ocean from East Africa to Australia.

The one positive aspect to Sino-Indian relations is the steady growth of trade, which could top $40 billion this year and could grow to $60 billion by 2010. China might become India's largest market replacing the U.S.

Random Views of Asia from the Mid-Pacific

William E. Sharp, Jr.

Chapter Eight

CENTRAL ASIA

Central Asia: Russia out, China in
Honolulu, March 12, 2006

The independent Central Asian "stans," Tajikistan, Kazakhstan, Kyrgyzstan, and Uzbekistan, were long obscured from global view when they were individual republics of the Soviet Union. As independent nations, they are now of great interest to China, which is quietly and persistently seeking political leadership in the region through the Chinese dominated Shanghai Cooperation Organization (SCO).

Historically, China played a dominant role in Central Asia with the mountainous desert region sending its tributaries to the Beijing court to pay homage. Central Asia has always been the global confluence of advanced East and West cultures and economies. After all, this is the area through which the Silk Road runs. Owing to a faltering Qing Dynasty and ineffectual Republic of China, Russian influence was only paramount during the last 100 years. Financially weakened and with its attention focused on Chechnya, Moscow's influence continues to atrophy. Chinese policy seeks regional leadership to eclipse U.S. influence, enhance the security of its Xinjiang Autonomous Region, to access oil and natural gas resources, and to increase investment and trade opportunities.

In 1991, Central Asian states declared independence from Russia and were immediately recognized by China. As Soviet republics, establishing international boundary lines with China was not a problem. To resolve international border demarcation problems, the Shanghai Five was established in 1991 consisting of Tajikistan, Kazakhstan, Kyrgyzstan, Russia, and China. Such issues were quietly and successfully settled. Then, in 2001, the Shanghai Five was transformed into the SCO and added Uzbekistan as a member state. A Chinese dominated organization housed in a modern, shiny glass building in Beijing's Chaoyang District, the SCO is dedicated to resolving multilateral issues of concern to member states. That is preventing separatism, extremism, terrorism, drug smuggling, and the spread of American influence. The SCO Secretary General is Zhang Deguang, a highly experienced, senior Chinese diplomat who has served in the Chinese Embassy in Washington, D.C. and as Ambassador to both Kazakhstan and Russia.

Once known as Chinese Turkistan and located in China's northwestern most corner, Xinjiang (the new border) is the home of China's Uighur minority. The Uighurs who trace their ancestry to Turkey are envious of the independence that their Muslim brothers in Central Asia enjoy. And many in Central Asia, including over 300,000 Uighurs dispersed throughout the region, want to see Xinjiang become independent East Turkistan. Uighur freedom fighters have received terrorist training in Central Asia. Once trained, they find their way through porous borders to Xinjiang to promote independence and the formation of a fundamentalist Islamic state often by bombing buses and markets. As a result, over four hundred people have died between 1990 and 2001. Given the inherent political instability in China proper, China is constantly concerned about unrest in Xinjiang where major weapons caches have been discovered. Moreover, the number of Muslim rebels has grown to the point where over 250,000 or one-tenth of People's Liberation Army soldiers are stationed in the autonomous region to ensure law and order, according to Swedish scholar Niklas Swanström's "China and Central Asia: A New Great Game or Traditional Vassal Relations?" in the November 2005 issue of the *Journal of Contemporary China*.

China is forever fearful of being geographically encircled by the U.S.; however, when the U.S. military entered Afghanistan, China overcame its fear and supported U.S. objectives. China reasoned that the U.S. presence in Afghanistan would be short and would help to eliminate the Taliban, which in turn would help to make China more secure. For once, China and America had a goal that they could cooperatively solve: the eradication of terrorism. However, as America enthusiastically turned to promoting democracy in Afghanistan, it was clear that their stay wouldn't be short. The Chinese became more and more concerned as demonstrators took to the streets in the Ukraine, Georgia, and nearby Kyrgyzstan demanding democracy. Chinese and American policy began to diverge. For their part, most SCO leaders are not only secular but also authoritarian. They have little if any interest in being lectured by American officials about promoting democracy. Moreover, given that many Central Asian state leaders were one-time Communist party leaders, they share a number of ideological perspectives with the Chinese.

Chinese President Hu Jintao declared that Central Asia is crucial to Chinese economic development. In fact, much of Chinese foreign policy is driven by the need to create a secure supply of natural resources to keep China's development moving forward. Central Asian states offer abundant reserves of oil, natural gas, and other natural resources. The recently completed Kazakhstan-China pipeline is a Chinese victory in the contest for control of Central Asian energy. Furthermore, Central Asia offers a convenient location for building a land-based, well protected pipeline from Iran and other Middle East oil producing countries through Central Asia into Xinjiang and onto China's heavily populated, coastal industrial centers. Such a pipeline would offer a system of transporting oil secure from U.S. naval and air forces that can interdict sea routes extending from the Middle East, through the Straits of Malacca, and north to Chinese ports. Moreover, the region is a good market for Chinese goods and other business deals, which will reap economic benefit for Xinjiang and China's Sichuan Province. To enhance its access to natural resources and to cultivate the market, China's "yuan diplomacy" has kicked into high gear making one loan of $5.7 million to Kyrgyzstan and another loan of $5 million to Tajikistan to buy Chinese products. While the countries are certainly glad to receive the loans, tying them to the purchase of Chinese goods might hurt China in the long run.

Spearheaded by the SCO, China's clout in Central Asia is growing while Russia's longstanding influence is receding. On the other hand, America's Central Asian influence is mainly concentrated in Afghanistan, having been asked to leave Uzbekistan's Karshi-Khanabad Air Base for pressuring the host government to democratize. That does not mean that there are no obstacles to Chinese policy success. Tenuous political stability in China proper is evident as the number of large scale domestic protests continues to grow and require lethal force to quell. Central Asian states are not always in agreement on transregional policies and play China off against Russia, when to their advantage. However, it is Japan that offers the greatest challenge to China in Central Asia. According to Christopher Len's "Japan Brings Balance to Central Asia" in the February 16, 2006 edition of *Asia Times Online*, Japan has given more than $2 billion U.S. dollars to foster long-term economic and social change in the region. Area officials do not see Japan as being primarily interested in the acquisition of natural resources. Compared to the Shanghai Cooperation Organization, the Central Asia Plus Japan Initiative, Japan's counter regional organization, is far less visible. While

Turkmenistan is not a SCO member and maintains a neutral foreign policy, it has joined the Japanese sponsored organization. Despite the role of both regional organizations, Central Asian states are fundamentally interested in their own well-being. Free of China's policy to tie economic assistance to protecting Chinese security concerns, Japanese policy enjoys the advantage of focusing on economic development. Japan can help to counterbalance both Chinese and residual Russian influence.

China's use of the SCO to achieve regionalization in Central Asia is further evidence of its move from a diplomacy based purely on bilateral relationships to one founded on multilateral relationships, in order to enhance its security and ensure access to natural resources. Having not yet achieved the degree of success it would like, China continues to cultivate the Association of Southeast Asian Nations. In Northeast Asia, the future of China's proposal to create a regional security system remains unknown. Of all three regional pursuits, China has been the most successful in Central Asia.

William E. Sharp, Jr.

Chapter Nine

VIETNAM

Beware: The Similarities are Growing
Honolulu, May 9, 2004

Senator John McCain is wrong! Vietnam and Iraq do share a striking set of similarities.

The initial logic for U.S. involvement in Vietnam and Iraq was based on faulty analysis. U.S. officials felt that they had to defeat Communism in Vietnam or else a global domino effect would ensue, resulting in other poor Third World countries turning to Communism. The U.S. lost in Vietnam, but no dominos fell. Just where are the weapons of mass destruction, and the conclusive proof that Iraq maintained any operational relationship with Al Qaeda? Dictators simply do not cozy up to uncontrollable, well-armed groups who are idealistically motivated and well financed.

America further justified its Vietnam involvement on the pretext of building democracy. However, the U.S. scuttled the 1956 Vietnamese election that would have unified Vietnam. Elections held by the Republic of Vietnam were one candidate farces, simply set up to allow the U.S. to show critics it was building democracy.

Likewise, it is obvious that the U.S. will have its fingerprints all over any Iraqi election and go to any length to have Ahmed Chalabi, Secretary Rumsfield's favorite, elected President.

The Department of Defense's belief in its technical superiority, conventional tactics, and earth shaking fire power made entering both conflicts seem less risky. Exposed to massive B-52 strikes, Viet Cong (VC) guerrillas simply went underground in their Chu Chi subterranean city until bombing stopped. They then came out unscathed and resumed fighting. In Iraq, U.S. technical superiority has done little to stem the growing frequency of highly effective small group operations. For example, the success of anti-American forces in cutting off re-supply routes and the siege at Fallujah. Despite the millions of dollars that has been invested in high tech weaponry, Iraqi insurgents, as the VC did before them, use the simple, inexpensive RPGs (rocket propelled grenade) with astonishing success. Shamefully, American soldiers and marines are still equipped with the M-16, which continues to frequently jam, just as it did in Vietnam nearly fourty years ago.

The U.S. and South Vietnamese governments had little chance to achieve victory once they lost the crucial support of the Buddhist establishment. The repeated self-immolation of Buddhist monks cost the U.S. and South Vietnamese government the broad popular support they desperately had tried to cultivate. Having been a key pillar of Saddam Hussein's support, it is no surprise that Iraq's Sunnis form a strong core of resistance against the

U.S. The U.S. hopes to cultivate the majority Shiite community, yet its actions clearly demonstrate the U.S. is trying to create an election system that will drastically limit Shiite political influence. No wonder we are witnessing growing cooperation between the two Islamic sects.

To many, Vietnam was a civil war, and currently, the biggest fear in Washington is that Iraq will become a civil war. Interestingly, both are bastardized countries, geographically configured by external powers. Iraq was cobbled together by the British in the early 1920s, combining the Kurds, Sunni, and Shiites. It is all too obvious that the Kurds would like to have their own homeland, and the Shiites are rumored to want a political hook up with Iranian Shiites. It is no wonder that Iraq required a strong man to hold it together. France stitched together Tonkin, Annam, and Cochin China to create Vietnam. Many see the Vietnam War as a civil war growing out of its traditional subdivisions. In fact, regional and ethnic animosities are still apparent in contemporary Vietnam.

The public supports the war, but then again they also did in the beginning of America's longest war.

Bright Shining Lie II
Honolulu, December 2, 2004

Throughout my life, I have been a strong supporter

of the military and am very comfortable with the U.S. as the pre-eminent world power. Such pre-eminence brings untold economic advantages and prestige to all Americans. Having lived abroad for a significant period of my life, I realize that while international politics is often wrapped in the sophistication and formality of an embassy cocktail party, it is more often a bare knuckles game of "he who has the most power, wins." Call it Darwinism or survival of the fittest. Nevertheless, a country cannot flaunt its power about in a non-collaborative manner in order to maintain its international supremacy and to avoid domestic discord. The Bush administration clearly crossed that line by invading Iraq.

Like many, I fell prey to the logic and rhetoric of the "Domino Theory." That notion held if the U.S. did not use its power to shore up the government of the Republic of Vietnam, that every other country in Southeast Asia would become Communist. American military power, technology, and democracy would save Vietnam. During my two years of service in Vietnam, I reluctantly concluded that democracy would not save Vietnam. Why? Democracy had no roots in Vietnam and was understood by very few Vietnamese. Moreover, what was supposed to pass as free and open elections were generally public relations ploys managed and manipulated by the Vietnamese government to make the Americans feel good about their presence in the country. Those that understood democracy—the educated—did not vote because they could easily see through the histrionics. Nevertheless, the U.S. government kept up the "let's democratize them" war chant, just as it is now doing in Iraq. The feeling of many Americans at the time was wrapped up in the book, *Bright Shining Lie,* by John Paul Van.

Witnessing the vast number of protesters in Berkeley's People's Park celebrating the North Vietnamese victory still inflames me. Such demonstrations illustrated the lack of expressive patriotism during the sixties and cynicism about government that I found so appalling. At heart, I have always been a flag waver and had trouble understanding why so few displayed the flag until days just after 9/11. In the ashes of 9/11, a new fire of patriotism was ignited and flags were found proudly waving in front of houses, from condo lanais, and atop cars. Flags of every dimension were on sale in just about every store, as were flag adorned baseball hats, sweatshirts, and tee shirts. I reveled in this tsunami of patriotism and quickly decorated my car, my office space, and classroom with both American flags and the yellow American Revolutionary War era flag embroidered with the head of a coiled snake in the attack position and the slogan "Don't Tread On Me." I felt a new, strong, titanic coming together of America, more intense than any other time in my lifetime.

Unfortunately, the wonderful spirit of patriotism Americans manifested quickly began to be abused. Marketers soon wrapped every product in a flag. Bruce Springsteen jumped on to the bonanza and came out with a "patriotic" album, *The Rising*. Newly burgeoning patriotism allowed politicians to advance policies and make statements that were more often than not simplistic in nature and void of reason. Reasoning was either "black" or "white." The "gray zone" also fell victim to 9/11. For President Bush, it was an especially simple matter, "Either you are for us, or you're against us." Very few dared to question the President or his administration because that was "unpatriotic," and, if you did question, you were not only unpatriotic, but you were also guilty of not supporting the troops. On the contrary, to question government power is the essence of democracy and to accept all government decisions is not to support the troops.

Like other Americans, I savored the destruction of the Taliban and hoped for the extermination of Osama Bin Laden. America—the world's largest safe haven, free of the omnipresent armed guards with large sections of communities enclosed with concertina wire, that I have seen in other countries, where people generally feel free to walk the streets, where warm summers drive out throngs of parents to the neighborhood baseball field to watch their children play and then head home to the serenity of their backyard to have fun-filled, care-free barbecues seemed to have been gunned down by nineteen angry Middle Easterners. Clearly! Undeniably! Osama is a mortal enemy of the U.S., but did we ever stop to analyze why? No, he suddenly became a handle to garner dwindling poll support for Bush prior to 9/11. Quickly and deliberately, Osama was spun into Hitler by the White House and Washington "news smiths." Yes, we should know about Hitler who was far worse than Osama, and then look at exactly what it is that spawned the popularity of Osama, so we can prevent more Osamas. You do not simply get to be a Osama, if you have not touched people.

There is no military solution to Osama or anyone like him. Despite their vast military power, in over ten years the Russians were unable to mold Afghanistan in their own image and finally left in disgrace. Are we likely to do any better in molding Afghanistan to our liking? I think not. Nevertheless, the flags were flying and people did not want to ask the hard questions. In such an atmosphere, Washington decided it had to keep beating the war drums and turned its attention to Iraq, a target that the neocons had been salivating over and itching to attack even before President Bush was elected. And if any one questioned U.S. motives or the likely success of military power, they were hastily and annoyingly reminded of the U.S. military's state of the art technology, despite its failure to catch Osama or get electricity again flowing in Baghdad.

We were supposed to have invaded Iraq because of "weapons of mass destruction" (WMD); however, to date none have been found. Then it was to democratize the Iraqis. But do they really want it? People in Iraq care about eating nutritious food, drinking fresh water, and generating electricity to power air-conditioners in 120 degree heat. Democracy is a luxury. If the U.S. so wants democracy in the Middle East, why was it so upset at the Turkish Parliament's democratically voted on decision to deny Turkish airspace to U.S. combat aircraft and to serve as a staging point for the 4th Infantry Division.

Why, if the U.S. is so concerned about democratizing Islamic countries, does it so embrace burgeoning dictatorships in Central Asia? Why does it chum up with a tottering dictatorship in Saudi Arabia, and why have we yet to see meaningful, promised democratic reforms in Kuwait? Certainly, it is difficult to consider Egypt and Jordan democracies. In the Western world, a product of the type of occupation that the U.S. wants to develop in Iraq, Germany refused to militarily join with the U.S. in Iraq. German Chancellor Schroeder was democratically re-elected on the promise that he would not send German troops to Iraq. He stood by his promise. Now, Bush avoids Schroeder and it is obvious that he will not get an invitation to the "ranch." To just what degree did oil play a motivating factor in Iraq? Or, for that matter, how much did oil underlie American support for Central Asian dictators given that lucrative pipelines will one day likely run through the region? Does oil explain U.S. "friendship" with the Saudi monarchy? Given the coziness of the administration with the oil and energy industries, *oil* is a clear motive.

Why was Saddam considered such a bad guy before the invasion? He was just as tyrannical when he was our buddy. There are other leaders just as heinous as Saddam, but we show no interest in removing them. If we were so morally outraged by his mass killings, why did we not seek to do something before? Even if he did have chemical, biological and even nuclear weapons, what were his intentions to use them? Many countries around the world have a full range of WMD, but they have no intention of using them other than in a defensive action.

Found or not, the WMD will be the centerpiece of every political speech before the November 2004 election. After all, 9/11 pumped life into a sagging Bush administration and allowed him to play the "war card" to obscure his lackluster performance and stodgy economy in hope of being re-elected. The photo opportunity of the one time Texas Air National Guard pilot, who never attended a guard meeting after completing flight training, landing on the deck of an aircraft carrier, before addressing sailors, is clear illustration of the image he wishes to convey to extend his stay at 1600 Pennsylvania Avenue.

Richer Brother, Poorer Brother
Honolulu, September 10, 2006

Both Vietnam and North Korea are among a handful of remaining "fraternal" Communist countries that grew out of colonialism and had to fight the U.S. along the way. Yet, a closer look at both reveals huge differences.

Vietnam has experienced little peace. Securing its independence from France in 1954, Vietnam soon found itself locked into war until 1975 when it finally defeated the U.S. backed Saigon government. Immediate post-war Vietnam was in terrible economic condition and suffered greatly due to a lack of food and medicine. In 1979, China invaded Vietnam in response to Vietnam's growing influence in Cambodia and Laos.

Upon the defeat of Japan, North Korea, officially called the Democratic People's Republic of Korea (DPRK), was established above the 38th parallel with the help of the Soviet Union. The 1950-1953 Korean War was an unsuccessful attempt by North Korea, China, and the Soviet Union to unify North Korea and South Korea under the control of the North. The Japanese left behind a reasonably advanced economy replete with industrial and hydroelectric power infrastructure and steel mills. The DPRK is endowed with such natural resources as coal, lead, tungsten, zinc, and graphite. Until the early 1960s, the North was considered more economically advanced than the South, which then began to launch an ambitious development plan.

The fall of the Soviet Union in late 1991 led to the withdrawal of Soviet aid that buoyed the Vietnamese economy. The Vietnamese government responded by instituting the "doi moi" (renovation) market based reforms that also brought limited political freedom. According to the August 5, 2006 edition of the *Economist*, during the period of 2001 to 2005, Vietnam's economy grew by 7.5%; in 2005, it grew by 8.4%. Coffee, a key Vietnamese crop, is vying with Brazil for the number one position in the global coffee market. Averaging various statistical data, less than 15% of the population is now considered poverty-stricken, making less than $1 a day; in 1990, the rate was 50%. The country is an attractive destination for foreign direct investment, having attracted close to $8 billion in 2005, with $2 billion coming from the U.S.

The Viet Kieu (overseas Vietnamese) remitted $6 billion in 2005 to support relatives still in the country. There is a growing trend for Taiwanese firms to pull their investments out of China and relocate them to Vietnam, which boasts a diligent work force that is 20% to 30% cheaper than China's. Intel is investing $300 million in an assembly plant in Ho Chi Minh City. Canon and Fujitsu are seriously considering investment in Vietnam. For those who still might be in doubt, Microsoft Chairman and CEO Bill Gates recently visited the country.

Developed by Kim Il Sung, the founder of the DPRK and father of the current president Kim Jong Il, the official ideology of the DPRK is "juche" or self-reliance. It is doubtful just how "self-reliant" North Korea has been throughout its existence. Kim Il Sung perfected the art of playing China off against the Soviet Union to get most of what he needed. With the Soviet collapse, all Russian aid stopped and starvation began to be a problem leading the North to depend on China for both fuel and food. Despite being closed to the outside world, North Korea began to accept food assistance from international organizations and even from nemesis South Korea. Nevertheless, despite urging from China, the North has failed to implement any meaningful economic reform for fear that it would dilute Stalinist political control.

Instead, the North has built an economy incorporating counterfeiting currency, producing and distributing illegal drugs, trading in missile technology, and depending on remittances from North Koreans living in Japan. It pays lip service to Chinese suggestions to adopt the type of economic policies that have helped both China and Vietnam, yet North Korea argues that China has abandoned Communism and lost its "spiritual" purity. North Korea is an inhospitable place to invest although it does allow some South Korean investment and trade.

With a population over 83 million, Vietnam's once mighty one million man and woman military now has 484,000 members sustained on a $650 million yearly military budget. There is no suggestion of acquiring or developing nuclear weapons. Vietnam's priority is economic growth, integrating into the global economy, and becoming a member of the World Trade Organization, which it will likely do in the near future. Vietnam wants the U.S. to remain engaged in the area. The population of the DPRK is approximately 23 million. Its one million strong military is supported by a $5 billion annual military budget. The military drains resources that would be better used in economic development as does nuclear weapon and missile development. The North would like the U.S. out of the South and Japan, if not Asia.

After Ho Chi Minh's death in 1969, Vietnam developed a system of collective leadership with no one figure monopolizing attention. It has maintained the ability to peacefully change leaders, although the selection process is limited to those at the highest levels of the Vietnamese Communist Party, the process does represent intra-party democracy. Moreover, Vietnam has displayed a certain flexibility to respond to limited popular input. Vietnamese leadership moves slowly, cautiously, and closely watches China's every move. The creation of the "Kim Dynasty" flies in the face of Communist doctrine which theoretically adheres to the abolition of feudalistic thought and practice. There is no intra-party democracy in Kim Jong Il's Korean Workers' Party or input from the people.

Vietnam has worked hard to build a more constructive relationship with the U.S. Former Prime Minister Phan Van Khai's June 2005 visit to the U.S. was the first time a leader of unified Vietnam visited the White House. U.S. House of Representatives Speaker, Dennis Hastert and Secretary of Defense Donald Rumsfeld have been to Vietnam. Vietnam has sent Vietnamese officers to attend military classes in the U.S. and is seriously considering volunteering troops to serve as UN peace keepers. Both countries are concerned about Chinese geopolitical intentions. North Korea and the U.S. maintain an antagonistic relationship that suffers from neo-conservative refusal to talk with Pyongyang and the idiosyncrasies of a shrewdly calculating despot, who has an unquenchable Donald Trump like need for media attention. The U.S. badly overplayed the China card thinking that China could get North Korea to stop nuclear weapon development. In reality, North Korea does not seem too concerned about China. Prior to the launching of seven missiles in July, China had unsuccessfully tried to persuade North Korea not to do so. Moreover, China has not been able to convince North Korea to return to the perennially stalled Six-Party Talks.

Vietnam is quietly and flexibly pursuing successful economic reforms and gradually joining the world community. North Korea is stubbornly and noisily adhering to its discredited economic policies and shows little interest in the world beyond its borders. The differences between the two brothers are stark, indeed.

Vietnam: Back on Track to Becoming a Tiger
Honolulu, March 8, 2009

Since the institution of *doi moi* (renovation) in 1986, Vietnam has impressed the world with its ideological flexibility in economically advancing the country. Everything seemed to be going swimmingly as Vietnam joined the World Trade Organization in 2007, making its entry onto the global economic stage official. In the view of many, it was only a matter of time before Vietnam would join Taiwan, South Korea, Singapore, and Hong Kong as the next economic Asian "tiger." Then, disaster struck as the stock market dropped, oil prices soared, corruption remained uncontrollable. It was obvious that Vietnam would not become the fifth Asian tiger, at least not quite as soon as hoped. Yet, with the same flexibility that had launched the country onto the global economic stage, Vietnam is working hard to capture the title it almost had.

After the American War (as the Vietnamese call the war with America) ended in 1975, life in Vietnam was very difficult economically. There was little food and medicine. To make matters worse, Vietnam had to beat off a Chinese invasion in 1979. Soon Vietnam hooked up with the Soviet Union. Following the Soviet model of economic development, Vietnam began the collectivization of agriculture, which by the early 80s was an obvious disaster. If there were any silver lining in the situation, Vietnam was pushed towards a market economy. From 1986, Vietnam was following the path of Doi Moi. As a result of the 1986 Congress of the Vietnamese Communist Party, Vietnam began to reach out to the world. In 1995, Vietnam joined the Association of Southeast Asian nations. In 2007, Vietnam joined the World Trade Organization and hosted the annual summit of the Asia-Pacific Economic Cooperation in Hanoi.

Annual growth had averaged 7.5% over the previous ten years. Upscale boutiques sprung up on both sides of Dong Khoi Street, which Vietnam veterans might remember as Tu Do Street, in the heart of Ho Chi Minh City. Coffee, rice, footwear, and clothing exports led a rising stream of Vietnamese exports. Moreover, millions were lifted out of poverty.

Vietnam was on a roll, but storm clouds were forming over the immediate horizon. Perhaps no one should have been surprised. In 1999, Vietnam specialists James Redel and William Turrey predicted the country's reform program would eventually lead to questions about political leadership and institutional viability. Their study further called for greater control over fiscal, monetary, and revenue matters. It also called for more transparency and accountability. It predicted the payments problem, accelerated inflation, and revenue loss that would trigger crisis.

They were right! In July, inflation was running at 28% with a year end average predicted to be between 25% and 30%. There was a balance of payments deficit of $15 billion in the first seven months of 2008. The stock market was down by 67%. Real estate prices were down in both Hanoi and Ho Chi Minh City. The price of rice had gone up 72.7% by July. The Asian Development Bank predicted a loss in Gross Domestic Product (GDP) from 7.0 to 6.5% or even a drop to 5%. Factory workers and the growing middle class were disheveled.

Prime Minister (PM) Nguyen Tan Dung rolled up his sleeves and sought to immediately manage the country's deteriorating situation. He accepted the advice of a board of foreign economic advisors by cutting subsidies to state owned enterprises, raised petroleum prices by 31%, and removed the cap on electricity prices letting them rise by 8.92%. Earlier this week, the PM announced a $17 billion package to stimulate the economy in view of the global financial situation.

While the PM has been aggressive, he faces certain political opposition within the Vietnamese Communist Party from conservative elders to those enjoying personal benefit from Vietnam's economic development. This is especially true where benefit is gained and authority is abused in the management of state owned enterprises, a large source of national debt. While Vietnam is more open and less authoritarian than China, many say that the economy will not truly move ahead until political liberty is completely unfettered.

Just as is the case in China, corruption remains a problem in Vietnam. In fact, Berlin-based Transparency International gives Vietnam a score of 2.7 on its 2008 Corruption Perceptions Index. Denmark, New Zealand, and Sweden get scores of 9.3. Out of 180 countries, the same three countries are ranked one, two, and three, respectively; Vietnam is ranked at 121. Corruption hinders Vietnam's ability to attract private foreign investment and aid. Japan, the largest donor of development aid, suspended assistance in December due to concern for corruption. Swedish Ambassador to Vietnam Rolf Bergman said, "The fight against corruption should be based on zero tolerance" and urged further action.

There is no doubt that Vietnam has an abundant supply of hard working cheap labor that undercuts the price of labor in China. However, Vietnam lacks the infrastructure that China has created. Products can be cheaply produced in Vietnam, but the problem occurs when transporting the product from the factory to a ship when rail links are limited and harbors are often not deep enough for large cargo ships. Vietnam has oil reserves but no refinery. Like other Asian countries, it has been too reliant on the U.S. market. Socioeconomically, there is growing gap between the rich and the poor, always an ominous sign especially for a country concerned with maintaining stability.

Nevertheless, the country offers boundless potential. Whereas China is an aging society, the average age in Vietnam is 25. Education standards are relatively high, and in Ho Chi Minh City and Hanoi, per capita income has surpassed $1,000, which is considered a key mile marker in developing a consumer society.

Even though Vietnam lost its opportunity to be crowned "tiger," the International Monetary Fund (IMF) and World Bank give the country two thumbs up. The IMF is impressed by Vietnam's central bankers who have rebuilt trust in the banking system, restored confidence in the "dong" (Vietnam's currency), and are successfully fighting inflation and credit problems by raising interest rates. All of this has helped to bring down food prices. The World Bank is impressed by how Vietnam works with donor countries and has achieved success in every project undertaken. It also believes the country will maintain a strong economic growth rate. A clear sign of confidence in Vietnam's economic future depends on whether Intel Corporation's plans to complete a one billion dollar factory, to open in Hanoi in 2010, remain in effect.

Resilience is the substance of Vietnam's national psyche. A nation that has fended off Chinese encroachment for much of its history, helped to defeat imperial Japan, dealt the coup de grace to French colonialism in Indo-China, and successfully countered American military power is back on track to becoming a tiger.

William E. Sharp, Jr.

Chapter Ten

RUSSIA

Russia's Manifest Destiny
Honolulu, August 13, 2006

Often confused with Siberia, the Russian Far East (RFE), in Russian "Dalny Vostok Rossii," lies in between Siberia and Russia's Pacific Coast forming the northeast corner of Asia. The taiga, tundra, and farmland topographically dominated RFE constitutes one-third of Russia's total land mass. With a population of seven million, representing over 25 ethnicities, the population density of one plus person per square kilometer is one of the lowest in the world.

Reminiscent of American westward expansion, the conquest of Siberia and the RFE is graphically portrayed in a telling painting in the Russian Museum in St. Petersburg depicting a Cossack officer brandishing his gleaming saber as he unmercifully cuts down a resisting native. Leading Russia's manifest destiny eastward of the Ural Mountains were hunters, trappers, run away serfs, and criminals who established small encampments and villages of ethnic Russians that soon began to multiply as the market for fur in European Russia grew.

Territorial expansion led to more territorial expansion at others' expense. In 1689, the first of what Chinese call the "unequal treaties," the Treaty of Nerchinsk was signed with the weak Ching Dynasty ruling China resulting in the loss of Outer Manchuria to Russia. From 1856 to 1857, Russia seized Chinese territory north of the Amur River (Heilongjiang in Chinese). A painting in the Khabarovsk Regional History Museum strikingly illustrates the signing of the Treaty of Aigun in 1858 between overly confident Russian Empire builder Count Nikolai Muravyov and a demure Ching Dynasty official. In 1860, all land east of the Ussuri River was ceded to Russia, extending Russia from the Baltic to the Pacific. As the Trans-Siberian Railroad continued expanding to hold European and Asian Russia together, more and more Russians transplanted themselves in the RFE.

In 1917, Japanese, U.S., British, and French forces arrived in Vladivostok hoping to prevent Germans from using the region's resources in its war effort and to support anti-Bolshevist forces led by Admiral Kolchak. Despite Kolchak's defeat and the departure of Allied troops, Japanese troops remained and, in 1920, created the Far Eastern Republic (FER) as a buffer against the Soviet Union. In 1922, the FER came to an end as Japanese troops left, and the area was incorporated into the Soviet Union.

Despite the ongoing natural gas bonanza in Sakhalin Island and even with an abundance of other natural resources including oil, iron ore, lignite, lead, zinc, silver, the Kolyma Gold Mines, lumber, farmland, and fish plus some iron and steel production, oil refining, and lumbering, the RFE has never been economically self-sufficient. As a result, the area has been highly reliant on subsidies from Moscow causing Russian President Vladimir Putin in 2002 to admonish area governors to reduce their dependence on Moscow's dole.

In the underpopulated, resource rich RFE, many residents feel abandoned by the distant Eurocentric government in Moscow, and neighboring China is seen as an economic and security threat. "Kitai" is the Russian word for China, which is said to be derived from "Khitan." The Khitan were originally a tribe from today's North and Northeastern China known for their warlike qualities. Mention of the RFE instantly elicits a Chinese response that the land is theirs: "It was stolen from them." A former translator in the Russian Ministry of Foreign Affairs is wary of Chinese intentions since they always refer to Khabarovsk and Vladivostok, the two principle cities in the RFE, by their respective Chinese names "Boli" and "Haisanwei," rather than by their Russian names.

Developed by the occupying Japanese in the 1930s and 1940s, Northeast China was one of China's key industrial centers as Mao Tse-tung assumed power on October 1, 1949. Rich in natural resources, the area abounded in steel mills and such heavy industries as the Red Flag Automobile Corporation. Times change. China's post-1978 economic development has mainly taken place in Beijing, Shanghai, the Pearl River Delta (between Hong Kong and Guangzhou), and in a few other places along the coast that offer speedy access to the sea.

China's two northern most provinces, Heilongjiang and Jilin, have no access to the sea. Now known as China's rust belt, unemployment could shortly reach 15% causing many of the 100 million residents to become politically restless. Normally considered a docile rubber stamp, the Chinese National People's Congress perfunctorily approves government policy. This year, Northeastern representatives to the Congress boldly reflected the people's concerns by calling out for economic remedies to be developed for the region. Given the economic plight of the area helps to explain why Falungong, a spiritual organization that masses have thronged to join looking for some escape from the travails of daily life, was founded in Northeast China.

Once a predominately Chinese city, Vladivostok is often compared to San Francisco because it is situated on a series of hills overlooking a bay. Stalin's ethnic cleansing of the 1930s emptied the city of its Chinese population. Today, resurgent Chinese influence can be seen in the 100,000 Chinese tourists who annually visit the city where they can legally gamble. A growing number of Chinese have become Russian citizens or have permanent residence, and the long, porous Sino-Russian border abets growing illegal Chinese immigration. In 2002, Chinese invested an estimated $200 million in restaurants, hotels, and other real estate in the RFE. Wishing to remain anonymous, a director of a well known Khabarovsk museum welcomed the money into the RFE; others are not as sanguine and fear Chinese take over. To increase the size of the population, immigration of ethnic Russians from former Soviet republics is strongly encouraged. To protect Russian natural resource wealth, in 2002, the Russian parliament triumphed in preventing the China National Petroleum Corporation (CNPC) from acquiring Slavneft, a major Russian oil producer. When it withdrew its bid, the CNPC was willing to pay 75 percent ($1.3 billion) more than the winning Russian tender.

Besides being likened to San Francisco, Vladivostok is often called "Russia's Dodge City" because of its often raucous, out of control reputation. In 2003, the entire RFE had the worst per person crime rate in the country according to Russian Minster for Internal Affairs Boris Gryzlov in an interview with Bertil Linter in *Asia Pacific Media Services Limited*. Luckily, streets are now a lot safer than in the early 90s when crime bosses were in control. In those days, smuggling, kidnappings, drive by shootings, and car bombings were every day events. Komitet Gosudarstvennoy Bezopasnosti, Committee for State Security or KGB-types never much cared for crime syndicates, so it was not surprising that former KGB operative Putin cracked down on organized crime. However, better organized Chinese triads (organized crime gangs) have taken the place of their Russian counterparts, and thrive on the civil order that Putin has created plus existent police and local government corruption.

Once considered the strongest of the five fleets in the Russian Navy, the Pacific Fleet (PF) is headquartered in

Vladivostok with additional ports throughout the RFE. Various estimates of the fleet's strength average out to fifty submarines, sixty-five surface vessels, and two hundred combat aircraft. Personnel strength is estimated at sixty thousand. Like the U.S. Pacific Command, headquartered at Camp Smith, the PF's area of operation is huge, running north to the northernmost coast of Russia, south to the Straits of Malacca, and east into the Western Pacific. During Soviet times, the PF also commanded the Russian Indian Ocean Squadron. Due to post-Soviet cost saving measures, men and material have been cut back. Russian navy vessels don't train as much as in Soviet days, and Sovremenny class destroyers designed "to kill" U.S. aircraft carriers can often be found tied up close to PF Headquarters. Nevertheless, the PF has carried out joint training exercises with the Chinese, Indian, and U.S. navies.

Vladivostok, like Honolulu, enjoys the economic benefits of a large military presence although they are not as plentiful as before. Luckily for the PF and Vladivostok, Russian Navy financing is growing although the navy has not yet created a workable doctrine attuned to today's world and contemporary Russia. Nor has Russia determined the nature of the more prominent role it is reported to desire in East Asia. According to Dr. Rouben Azizian, a Russian specialist at the Asia-Pacific Center for Security Studies, Russia's evolving role is focused on "supplying arms to China, India, and hopefully Association of Southeast Asian Nation members; marketing energy amidst all of the competition for its resources; and operating in a multilateral fashion through such organizations as the Shanghai Cooperation Organization, rather than just carrying out foreign policy based on bilateral relations."

Like Russia itself, the RFE has not really chartered a clear role for its future. It lacks a sense of what its economic life should be. It is handicapped in achieving such a sense due to its demographic problems, corruption, fears about China, the uncertain direction of the Russian government, and the nature of its relationship with Moscow. Until satisfied, such concerns will make it difficult to establish more economically cooperative relations with bordering Asian countries, which is felt to be a long-term solution to achieving more prosperous times.

Random Views of Asia from the Mid-Pacific

Afterward

Since this work was originally written, America's position in Asia has become clearer. President Obama is known as the "Pacific President." United States Secretary of State Hillary Rodham Clinton left no doubt breaking with tradition and making her first official trip abroad to Asia, rather than to Europe. Realizing that Asia had felt overlooked during the administration of George W. Bush, she said the administration wants to "develop a broader and deeper relationship" with Asia. America will continue to play a key role in Asia and fears to the contrary should all be assuaged. Realistically, we know that our relationships with Asia will impact our own future.

More and more, the center of the world tilts towards Asia, especially as China continues its climb to economic and military great power status. Yet, despite morphing the country into a global manufacturing hub and lifting millions out of poverty, China lacks a compelling universal value. Demonstrators in Egypt, Tunisia, Libya and other Middle Eastern countries seek to create Western democratic systems, more akin to Taiwan, Japan, India, and South Korea, while replacing totalitarian regimes that share many coercive characteristics with China. The same can be said about political dissidents in Myanmar (Burma), an Asian country right on China's door step. China continues to support not only Myanmar but also such unsavory regimes as North Korea, Sudan,

Zimbabwe, and others.

In all of this, America has created a China policy which seeks to encourage the participation of China in an international system where human rights are valued; where there is freedom of navigation, robust free and fair trade, and shared responsibility for addressing global problems. Nevertheless, America has hedged its policy by increasing its security commitments to Asia. Asian countries seek a stronger American security commitment and presence in Asia as an insurance policy against potential Chinese regional hegemony.

While addressing Asian concerns for a stronger security commitment, the United States must never forget that Asia has grown up. Unlike in the past, the U.S. cannot simply dictate to Asian leaders; it must follow a more consultative and collaborative approach to leadership while further encouraging a shared sense of responsibility. It must also have the flexibility to function bilaterally and multilaterally or if need be unilaterally.

The U.S. must do all it can to pursue a good relationship with China. A good U.S.-China relationship is vital to the well-being of the Asia-Pacific region and beyond. However, the United States must never forget its commitments to Taiwan or be deluded into thinking that diluting its relationship will somehow resolve U.S.-China relations. As a Chinese journalist once said, "There will always be problems in the U.S.-China relationship due to the differences in political and economic systems."

William E. Sharp, Jr.

Random Views of Asia from the Mid-Pacific

About the Author

William E. Sharp, Jr. began his association with Asia in 1968 while serving with U.S. Army military intelligence in Vietnam. He has an B.A. Degree in Political Science focused on Chinese and Japanese politics from the University of California, Berkeley. In Hawaii, he received an M.A. Degree in Asian Studies from the University of Hawaii at Manoa along with the James Shigeta Award for Excellence in Asian Studies and the Lee-Shao Chang Award for Excellence in Chinese Studies. He has studied Mandarin Chinese in both Taipei and Beijing. During the 1980s, he lived in Japan where he taught English and worked as a free-lance writer. Returning to the U.S. in 1989, he attended Harvard University where he earned an Ed.M. (Master of Education) Degree in Administration, Planning, and Social Policy. In the early 1990s, he served as Executive Director of the Japan-America Society of Hawaii. He currently teaches classes about East Asian politics at Hawaii Pacific University and hosts *Asia in Review*, a weekly TV show dedicated to substantive discussion of contemporary Asian affairs. From late 2005 to early 2009, he wrote "Look East," a column for the *Honolulu Star-Bulletin* on Asian affairs. He often travels to Asia.

If you enjoyed *Random Views of Asia from the Mid-Pacific* consider these other fine Books from Savant Books and Publications:

A Whale's Tale by Daniel S. Janik
Tropic of California by R. Page Kaufman
The Village Curtain by Tony Tame
Dare to Love in Oz by William Maltese
The Interzone by Tatsuyuki Kobayashi
Today I am a Man by Larry Rodness
The Bahrain Conspiracy by Bentley Gates
Called Home by Gloria Schumann
Kanaka Blues by Mike Farris
First Breath edited by Zachary M. Oliver
Poor Rich by Jean Blasiar
The Jumper Chronicles by W. C. Peever
William Maltese's Flicker by William Maltese
My Unborn Child by Orest Stocco
Last Song of the Whales by Four Arrows
Perilous Panacea by Ronald Klueh
Falling but Fulfilled by Zachary M. Oliver
Manifest Intent by Mike Farris
Mythical Voyage by Robin Ymer
Hello, Norma Jean by Sue Dolleris
Richer by Jean Blasiar
Charlie No Face by David B. Seaburn
Number One Bestseller by Brian Morley
My Two Wives and Three Husbands by S. Stanley Gordon
In Dire Straits by Jim Currie
Wretched Land by Mila Komarnisky
Chan Kim by Ilan Herman

William E. Sharp, Jr.

Who's Killing All the Lawyers? by A. G. Hayes
Ammon's Horn by G. Amati
Wavelengths edited by Zachary M. Oliver
Almost Paradise by Laurie Hanan
Communion by Jean Blasiar and Jonathan Marcantoni
The Oil Man by Leon Puissegur

Scheduled for Release in 2012:

In the Himalayan Nights by Anoop Chandola
Blood Money by Scott Mastro
The Isla Vista Crucible by Reilly Ridgell
Perverse by Larry Rodness
On My Behalf by Helen Doan
Rules of Privilege by Mike Farris

http://www.savantbooksandpublications.com

www.ingramcontent.com/pod-product-compliance
Lightning Source LLC
Chambersburg PA
CBHW071653090426
42738CB00009B/1510